Confirmation

Allen, Texas

"The Ad Hoc Committee to Oversee the Use of the Catechism, United States Conference of Catholic Bishops, has found this text, copyright 2007, to be in conformity with the *Catechism of the Catholic Church;* it may be used only as supplemental to other basal catechetical texts."

Sacrament Preparation Development Team

Developing a sacrament preparation program requires the talents of many gifted people working together as a team. RCL Benziger is proud to acknowledge these dedicated people who contributed to the development of this Confirmation preparation program.

Reverend Robert D. Duggan, STD
Author
Liturgical Advisor

Alan Talley
Writer, Catechist Guide

Rev. Louis J.Cameli, STD
Theological Advisor

Elaine McCarron, SCN, M Div.
Catechetical Advisor

Kate Sweeney Ristow
National
Catechetical Consultant

Steven Ellair
Patricia Classick
Project Editors

Jo Rotunno
Director of
Creative Development

Susan Smith
Managing Editor

Jenna Nelson
Production Director

Laura Fremder, Manager
Electronic Page Makeup

Lisa Brent, Director
Tricia Legault
Art and Design

Joseph Crisalli
A. C. Ware
Web Site Producers

Ed DeStefano
General Editor

Maryann Nead
President/Publisher

NIHIL OBSTAT
Rev. Msgr. Robert Coerver
Censor Librorum

IMPRIMATUR
† Most Rev. Charles V. Grahmann
Bishop of Dallas

August 22, 2006

The Nihil Obstat and Imprimatur are official declarations that the material reviewed is free of doctrinal or moral error. No implication is contained therein that those granting the Nihil Obstat and Imprimatur agree with the contents, opinions, or statements expressed.

Send all inquiries to:
RCL Benziger
200 East Bethany Drive
Allen, Texas 75002-3804

Toll Free   877-275-4725
Fax   800-688-8356

Visit us at **www.FaithFirst.com**
     www.RCLBenziger.com
Customer Service E-mail: **cservice@RCLBenziger.com**

Printed in the United States of America
by ColorDynamics, Allen, TX

20561   ISBN 978-0-7829-1139-8 (Candidate Book)
20562   ISBN 978-0-7829-1140-4 (Catechist Guide)
20563   ISBN 978-0-7829-1141-1 (Sponsor Handbook)

3 4 5 6 7 8 9 10 • 13 12 11 10 09 08

Contents

Welcome

Welcome to RCL's Confirmation preparation program. In one sense, you have been preparing for several years. As you know Confirmation is one of the three Sacraments of Christian Initiation, which are the foundation of the Christian life. You have already received the Sacrament of Baptism and the Eucharist. Now you are responding to the grace and invitation of God to prepare for and receive Confirmation and complete your initiation into the Church. Through the Sacrament of Confirmation, you will be united more closely with Christ, bound more firmly to the Church, strengthened with the gift of the Holy Spirit, and sent forth to spread the Good News. Each chapter of this book opens up the meaning of one aspect of the rite of Confirmation. This will help you both understand the rite and participate in it actively and fully and live the faith of the Church as a faithful and responsible witness for Christ.

As you begin your preparation for Confirmation, consider these reflections and write your initial responses. This reflection time will help you open your mind and heart to the preparation time you are now beginning. Throughout the preparation process, refer back to your responses occasionally to see if any of your responses have changed or you wish to add to your responses.

As I begin this preparation time, I understand the Sacrament of Confirmation to be

_____

_____

To live one's life as a witness for Christ means to

_____

_____

I will enter into this time of preparation fully by

_____

_____

My prayer for others who are also preparing to receive this sacrament is

_____

_____

chapter 1

Gathering as Church

Reflection on the Opening Ritual

What part of the opening ritual most helped you have a sense of God's presence with us? Why?

The people of Nazareth with whom Jesus gathered for prayer in the synagogue "looked intently at him . . . and were amazed at the gracious words that came from his mouth" (Luke 4:20–22). In our prayer together we too are sometimes awestruck at the knowledge that Jesus is with us and speaks gracious words to us whenever we gather in his name.

When have you gathered with others and been aware of Jesus' presence?

Gathering of participants, World Youth Day, Veltins Arena in Gelsenkichen, Germany, August 14, 2005.

The People of God

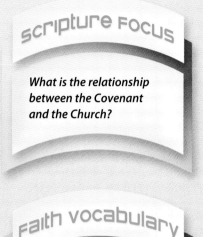
Covenant

The solemn agreement between God and his people in which they mutually committed themselves to each other; the new and everlasting Covenant was established in Jesus Christ through his Paschal Mystery—the saving mystery of his Passion, death, Resurrection, and Ascension—and the sending of the Holy Spirit on Pentecost.

Church

The People of God, whom God the Father has called together in Jesus Christ through the power of the Holy Spirit.

The Bible reveals that God has called a people together to be his people and has entered into a solemn agreement, called the **Covenant,** with them. The biblical account of the Covenant is the story of the solemn agreement between God and his people in which they mutually committed themselves to each other.

The Covenant in the Old Testament

The story of the Covenant begins at creation. It continues with the Covenant God made with Noah and all humanity (see Genesis 3:14–16, 9:9–17) and with the Covenant God entered into with Abraham, promising that Abraham would be the father of a great people. (See Genesis 12:1–3.)

Moses with the Ten Commandments. Domenic Mastrojanni, twentieth-century Italian painter.

In dramatic fashion, God brought Abraham's descendants, the Israelites, out of slavery from Egypt, led them through the desert, and entered into the Covenant with them at Mount Sinai, also called Mount Horeb. (See Exodus 19:4–6.) In the Book of Deuteronomy, Moses reminds the Israelites what God has done for them by gathering them together as the People of God. Moses tells the people:

> "There was the day on which you stood before the LORD, your God, at Horeb. . . . He proclaimed to you his covenant, which he commanded you to keep."
>
> DEUTERONOMY 4:10, 13

From that day forward, the Israelites, or Jewish people, have regularly gathered together to renew their commitment to live the Covenant by obeying the Commandments God gave them.

The New and Everlasting Covenant

The early **Church** recognized that the same God who gathered the Israelites to be his people had now called them to be his people in a new Covenant. The beginning, or salutation, of many of the New Testament letters of Saint Paul speaks to the nature of the Church as the people called together by God in Christ. In the salutation of the First Letter to the Corinthians, Paul writes:

> Paul, called to be an apostle of Christ Jesus by the will of God, and Sosthenes our brother, to the church of God that is in Corinth, to you who have been sanctified in Christ Jesus, called to be holy, with all those everywhere who call upon the name of our Lord Jesus Christ, their Lord and ours.   1 CORINTHIANS 1:1–2

St. Paul Preaching at the Areopagus, detail from wool tapestry. Raphael (1483–1520), Italian painter and architect.

The writers of the New Testament often use the Greek word *ekklesia* to name the people whom God has gathered in Jesus Christ, the Incarnate Son of God, who is true God and true man. They gave this Greek word, which originally referred to any convocation, gathering, or assembly of people, a new and unique meaning.

The word *ekklesia* specifically described their identity as the Church. The Church is the People of God whom God the Father has called together in Jesus Christ through the power of the Holy Spirit. Christ dwells within the Church, rules over her, and continues to work through her.

How do Paul's words describe the Church?

lifelinks

In a small group discuss how God works through the people of your parish. List your thoughts. Then describe a parish activity in which you could participate with others.

_____

_____

_____

The Body of Christ

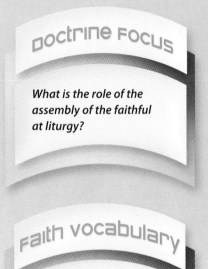

Faith Vocabulary

liturgy

The participation of the People of God in the "work of God"—the work of the whole Church, of Christ the Head of the Church, and of the members of the Body of Christ through which Christ continues the work of Redemption.

When immigrants apply for and receive citizenship in the United States of America, they acquire the identity of those citizens. This newly acquired identity brings with it many rights and responsibilities. How citizens do or do not exercise those rights and fulfill those responsibilities affects America and all her people.

A Holy Nation, A Royal Priesthood

The First Letter of Peter recognizes that all those baptized into Christ constitute a group that has a unique identity. We read, "You are 'a chosen race, a royal priesthood, a holy nation, a people of [God's] own'" (1 Peter 2:9). Reflecting on this passage, the Church has come to understand that we worship God as a people whom God the Father has gathered together in Christ. At the Second Vatican Council, the bishops taught that when the assembly of the baptized faithful gathers for the **liturgy,** Christ is with them:

> Christ is *always present in his Church* [emphasis added] especially in her liturgical celebrations. . . . He is present in the Sacrifice of the Mass not only in the person of his minister . . . but especially in the eucharistic species. . . . He is present in his word. . . . Lastly he is present when the church prays and sings. . . ."
>
> THE CONSTITUTION ON THE SACRED LITURGY [SACROSANCTUM CONCILIUM] 7

It is with Christ and through Christ and in Christ and through the power of the Holy Spirit that the faithful offer honor and glory to the Father as one people. God the Father is adored as the source of all the blessings of creation and salvation with which he has blessed us in his Son so we may become his adopted children.

The Assembly of the Faithful

On the day of your Confirmation, the Church will gather around the bishop or the priest delegated by him. The bishop, the priests of your parish and your catechist, your family and sponsor, the other ministers and the assembly will gather and join with you. Confirmation, of course, would be validly administered if only the bishop, or the priest delegated by him,  were there to confirm you. They represent the Church and act in the name and Person of Christ. The bishop is a successor of the Apostles and, in communion with the Pope, governs the Church.

The simple presence of the assembly, however, is not enough. It is not only important that we gather for the liturgy but also how we gather. The Church reminds us that "in order that the liturgy may be able to produce its full effects it is necessary that the faithful come to it with proper dispositions . . . and that they cooperate with heavenly grace lest they receive it in vain" (Constitution on the Sacred Liturgy 11).

Everyone will join in prayer, asking that the Holy Spirit be poured out on you. The place where you gather will be filled with believers, as Mary and the disciples filled the Upper Room on Pentecost.

Why is it important that the assembly of the faithful gather to participate in your Confirmation?

Liturgy Link

In the Order of the Latin Mass celebrated after the Council of Trent, the first line began with the words *Sacerdos paratus* ("When the priest is ready"). In the revised Order of the Mass approved for use after the Second Vatican Council, those opening words were changed to *Populo congregato* ("When the people have gathered"). This change in the revised Order of the Mass signals the vital role the assembly of the faithful has whenever the Eucharist and other sacraments are celebrated.

lifelinks

In a small group discuss the attitudes of mind and heart that a person needs to bring to the celebration of the liturgy. In this space record the list generated by your group.

_____

_____

_____

The Church Gathers

RITUAL FOCUS

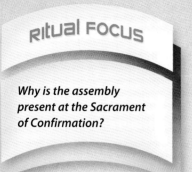

Why is the assembly present at the Sacrament of Confirmation?

Faith vocabulary

Body of Christ
An image for the Church used by Saint Paul the Apostle that teaches that all the members of the Church are one in Christ, the Head of the Church, and that all members have a unique and vital work in the Church.

sacrament
An "efficacious sign of grace, instituted by Christ and entrusted to the Church, by which divine life is dispensed to us through the work of the Holy Spirit" (*Catechism of the Catholic Church* 1131).

Some things that we do come so naturally that we are often not even aware of how significant these actions really are. For example, when some families pray grace before meals, family members may spontaneously join hands as a way of expressing their union in prayer. By that simple action the members of the family are saying, "This is who we are."

Gathering as the Body of Christ

There are many ritual actions that we use to celebrate the liturgy that come so naturally we often do not stop and think about their deeper meaning. One of those actions is when the Church assembles for liturgy. We do not gather on our own intiative. We respond to God's invitation. It is God who calls the assembly into being and it is the Holy Spirit who builds and sanctifies the Church.

In his letters Saint Paul reflected on the significance of the ritual actions of the Church and admonished Christians to be aware of their significance. For example, Saint Paul taught that the Church is the **Body of Christ** (see 1 Corinthians 12:12–31) and he admonished the Church in Corinth about the inappropriate and irreverent ways they were gathering and celebrating the Eucharist. Their behavior revealed that they had forgotten who they were and what they were celebrating. (See 1 Corinthians 11:17–34.)

The Church is the Mystical Body of Christ. She is both visible and spiritual, both human and divine. There is a profound unity that binds Christ and all the members of the Body of Christ, the Church. All the members of the Church are one in Christ, the Head of the Church.

Saint Paul preaching in Corinth, stone sculpture.

The celebration of the **Sacrament** of Confirmation begins with the gathering of the assembly of the faithful after which the Introductory Rites of the Mass begin. The *Rite of Confirmation* states: "When the candidates, their sponsors and parents, and the whole assembly of the faithful have gathered, the bishop [walks in procession] to the sanctuary with the priests who assist him, one or more deacons, and the ministers. Meanwhile all may sing a psalm or appropriate song" (Rite of Confirmation 34).

This directive, or rubric, for celebrating Confirmation reminds us that every celebration of the liturgy is "meant to be celebrated in common, with the faithful present and actively participating" (*Constitution on the Sacred Liturgy* 7, 27.) We join with Christ, the one, eternal, high Priest, who is the main celebrant of the liturgy. With him, we offer the prayers of the liturgy as the priestly People of God.

Your family and friends, and many members of your parish, will come together to celebrate with you on the day of your Confirmation. That gathering of the Church will be a sign that the Body of Christ, the priestly People of God, is present in a special way.

What does the gathering of the worshiping assembly signify?

lifelinks

In a small group discuss what you observe when people of your parish gather together for worship on Sunday. Describe what you see that tells about their understanding of themselves as the Body of Christ.

What I See	What It Says
_____	_____
_____	_____
_____	_____

The Church
Lives the Faith

Wonderful things can happen when people gather for a good purpose. For example, the Civil Rights Movement in the 1960s embraced a nonviolent philosophy. Its members relied heavily on the power of people gathering together to bear witness to the equal dignity of all people, to work against injustice, and to seek change within society and within the minds and hearts of Americans. Change began to happen as the size of those gatherings grew. More and more citizens began to take notice and take part in the movement.

Encounter the Gospel of Life

The Church also knows a great deal about the power of people gathering together and the difference that the power of such gatherings can make. In the late 1990s, a handful of youth ministers in the Archdiocese of Washington, D.C., dreamed of gathering youth and adults from various parishes to learn, reflect on, and put into practice Catholic Social Teaching. At first this gathering was held during a summertime weeklong "service camp." This gathering, known as Encounter the Gospel of Life, has grown to become a year-round process of formation and transformation. Hundreds of young people, their parents, and adults involved in youth ministry take part.

Following Christ's Command

The heart of the Encounter the Gospel of Life gathering is an intensive week of service with people in the Washington, D.C., area who are living in poverty or who experience needs in other ways. Soup kitchens, homes for the elderly, inner-city children's programs, and many other settings provide the opportunity, not only for doing Works of Mercy as Christ commanded in Matthew 25:31–46 and John 13:34–35, but just as importantly, for putting a human face on sisters and brothers in need.

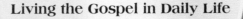

Living the Gospel in Daily Life

An exuberant atmosphere of learning about the connections between such good works and Catholic Social Teaching fills early morning prayer, afternoon conversations, and evening formation sessions. Songs, skits, dancing, witness talks, and many other engaging ways of exploring faith keep the camp participants focused and excited about what they are learning. Discovering the connections between the Eucharist and action for justice is one of the valuable outcomes that regularly characterizes the experience of both young and old alike.

Encounter the Gospel of Life is much more than a simple opportunity to lend a helping hand. It is a call to conversion. It is an invitation to a deepened faith and to a more intentional way of living the Gospel in daily life. You can learn more about Encounter the Gospel of Life at their Web site: www.eglweb.org.

What gatherings of Christians can you name that make a difference in our world today? Describe how each gathering makes a difference by putting the Gospel into action.

Living the Faith
Makes a Difference

Teens gather in a variety of ways. They spend their time in a variety of ways. How teens gather and how they spend their time reveals a great deal about them and makes a difference in their lives.

Spending Time with Friends

Researchers who study human growth and development have for a long time observed the tremendous influence that teens have on one another—especially those who "hang out" regularly with one another. While the movement of teens from spending time with families to spending more time with friend-centered groups, or peer groups, can sometimes be a source of distress and anxiety to parents, it is both a normal and essential developmental step for young people.

The growing role of peer groups in your life can be a blessing or a risk, depending on the values and behaviors that the friends you spend time with reinforce. Who you hang out with is part of your forming an identity as an independent person. Think about the friends with whom you regularly gather. The people with whom you regularly spend time can tell a great deal about who you think you are and what values you live by.

Spending Time Doing . . .

Researchers also study trends in how young people spend their time. One research study polled more than 2,500 teens and young adults. Research showed that in an average week, twelve- to twenty-four-year-old Americans spend 16.7 hours online, 13.6 hours watching television, 12 hours listening to the radio, 7.7 hours talking on the phone, and 6 hours reading books and magazines.

Such studies often come up with fascinating statistics. But for someone who wishes to be known as a disciple of Jesus Christ, these numbers call us to evaluate how we spend our time. Who do you enjoy hanging out with most? How much time do we spend with Christ? Where do you invest your time and energy in a given week? How much time do we consciously choose to live the Gospel?

Researchers often ask young people to keep a detailed diary of how they spend their time each day over a period of a week or two. What might such a diary tell you about yourself as a disciple of Jesus? About your priorities and your values and how they are based on the Gospel? What would your diary reveal about the role that faith plays in your life?

Faith Decision

- In a small group brainstorm the activities that you think teens spend their time doing.

- Once your group has developed its list, create two columns on a piece of paper. In one column write what you think is the average amount of time teens actually spend on each activity. In the other column write the amount of time that you think a responsible Christian teen might spend on that activity.

This week I will keep a personal log each day of how much time I spend living my faith. After reviewing my time log, I will

_____

_____

_____ .

In this chapter you learned about the liturgical action of gathering. You explored that the way we gather for worship as the Body of Christ reflects, in many ways, the values that shape our daily lives. You also discussed that where, how, and with whom we gather during the week helps to shape the attitudes and readiness that we bring as we gather for Sunday worship.

Reflect on the different groups with whom you have gathered and spent time this week. Write about how you greet others and welcome them into the groups. What more could you have done to make these gatherings a success?

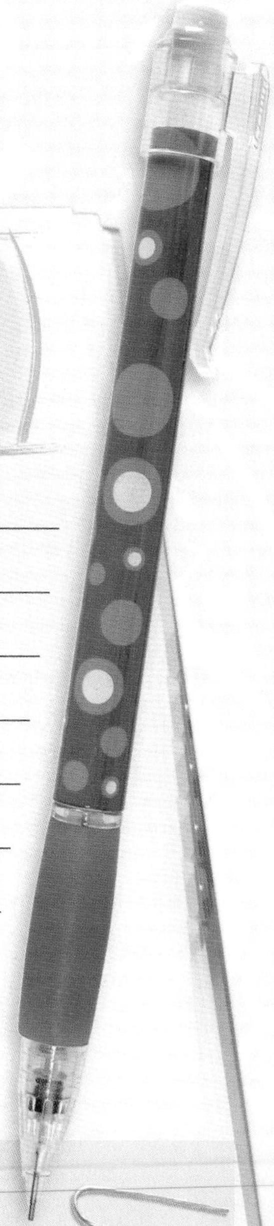

_____

_____

_____

_____

_____

_____

_____

_____

_____

_____

_____

A question to share with your sponsor and parents :

How well do you think our patterns of gathering, including how, where, for what, and with whom we gather, make us recognizable as Jesus' disciples?

Chapter 2
Proclaiming God's Word

Reflection on the Opening Ritual

Which reading or readings in the opening ritual caught your attention? Why?

Before the age of printing technologies, manuscripts and books were highly valued and treated with greater care and respect than they seem to be today. In times past the Bible was often decorated with original artwork as a sign of great honor and reverence for the Word of God. Today we tend to take less care of the printed Word of God. For example, we routinely throw away missalettes, which contain the Word of God proclaimed at Mass. We need to be careful that the mass printing of Bibles does not contribute to a lessening of our reverence that is due the printed Word of God.

How can we show respect and reverence for the printed Word of God?

The Word of the Lord

Faith Vocabulary

parable
A type of story that Jesus told comparing one thing to another to teach and invite his listeners to make a decision to live for the Kingdom of God.

Kingdom of God
The biblical image used to describe all people and creation living in communion with God when Jesus Christ comes again in glory at the end of time.

All of us have had times when we "tuned out" what someone was saying to us. This response may have occurred because we were distracted by something or someone else. Or perhaps we deliberately refused to listen because of negative feelings about the speaker or what was being said. Such inattentive and nonresponsive listening can have serious consequences. Saint Matthew's Gospel points out the tragic consequences of not listening attentively and responding to Jesus, the Incarnate Word of God.

The Parable of the Sower

Matthew's Gospel is organized around a series of narratives and sermons of Jesus. The third narrative and sermon, Matthew 11:1—13:1–52, contains a number of **parables** about the **Kingdom of God** and describes how the preaching of Jesus meets with growing resistance. The parable of the Sower (Matthew 13:1–9) comes from this third sermon in Matthew's Gospel and teaches the importance of listening to Jesus and not resisting his word.

Matthew begins the parable of the Sower with the seemingly unimportant detail of Jesus sitting down to speak to the crowds. Including this detail emphasized the importance of listening attentively to and not resisting the teacher. Sitting down was the posture taken by a teacher who spoke with authority.

Matthew writes that after Jesus got into a boat, he sat down and taught the crowd that was standing on the beach. After instructing them to listen he said:

> "A sower went out to sow. And as he sowed, some seed fell on the path, and birds came and ate it up. Some fell on rocky ground, where it had little soil. It sprang up at once because the soil was not deep, and when the sun rose it was scorched, and it withered for lack of roots. Some seed fell among thorns, and the thorns grew up and choked it. But some seed fell on rich soil, and produced fruit, a hundred or sixty or thirtyfold. Whoever has ears ought to hear." MATTHEW 13:3–9

The Fruit of Rich Soil

After Jesus finished speaking to the crowd, his disciples approached him privately and asked him about the meaning of the parable. Jesus replied:

"This is why I speak to them in parables, because 'they look but do not see and hear but do not listen or understand.' "

Jesus continued:

"The seed sown on the path is the one who hears the word of the kingdom without understanding it, and the evil one comes and steals away what was sown in his heart. The seed sown on rocky ground is the one who hears the word and receives it at once with joy. But he has no root and lasts only for a time. When some tribulation or persecution comes because of the word, he immediately falls away. The seed sown among thorns is the one who hears the word, but then worldly anxiety and the lure of riches choke the word and it bears no fruit. But the seed sown on rich soil is the one who hears the word and understands it, who indeed bears fruit and yields a hundred or sixty or thirtyfold." MATTHEW 13:13, 19–23

Parable of Sower, contemporary illustration, artist unknown.

What do the images of the sower and the seed help you understand about listening and responding to the Word of God?

lifelinks

Identify different circumstances that might distract you from listening and responding to the Word of God. List some of those distractions below. Then brainstorm changes that you could make in your listening habits to be more attentive in the future.

Distractions	Changes

God Speaks to Us

Faith Vocabulary

Divine Revelation
God's free gift of gradually, over time, communicating in words and deeds his own mystery and his divine plan of creation and Salvation.

biblical inspiration
The process by which the Holy Spirit assisted the human writers of Sacred Scripture so that they would teach faithfully, and without error, the saving truth that God, the principal author of the Scriptures, wished to communicate.

Sometimes when we meet someone, we are immediately attracted to that person and sense that we could become a good friend with that person. Conversation comes about very easily, and we quickly share stories about ourselves. But it can also happen that the other person is very shy. Sometimes the person does not "open up" and tell us about themselves. If people will not tell us about themselves, it is virtually impossible for any relationship to begin, grow, and develop.

God's Words and Mighty Deeds

God has told us much about himself. He has made known, or revealed, in words and deeds the mystery of who he is and his divine plan of creation and Salvation for humankind. The action of God "speaking" to us is called **Divine Revelation.** Through his Self-Revelation, God invites us to enter into relationship with him. In the New Testament we read:

> In times past, God spoke in partial and various ways to our ancestors through the prophets; in these last days, he spoke to us through a son, whom he made heir of all things and through whom he created the universe. HEBREWS 1:1–2

Jesus Christ is the final and definitive Word of God. He is the only Son of God the Father who became incarnate, assuming human nature without losing his divine nature. After Jesus Christ there is no further Revelation.

The Holy Spirit, Teacher and Advocate

Divine Revelation is passed on both in Sacred Scripture and in Sacred Tradition. Sacred Tradition is the "living memory" and "living transmission" of God's truth with the assistance of the Holy Spirit among the People of God in every generation. It is the ministry of the Church to grasp, over time, the meaning and significance of Divine Revelation.

Biblical inspiration is the term the Church uses to name the Holy Spirit's action of assisting the human writers of Sacred Scripture so that they faithfully and without error communicate the saving truth that God wanted to share. It is through the action of the same Holy Spirit that the Church, through her Magisterium, authentically interprets and faithfully hands on "the Word of God, whether in its written form or in the form of Tradition" (*Catechism of the Catholic Church* 85).

God has freely spoken his word and invites us to listen and respond because he wants us to live in friendship and communion with him. He wants us to know him and love him and serve him. This is why it is so vital that we listen attentively to the Word of God proclaimed at Mass and respond in a way that deepens our relationship with him. When this happens, we are "good soil." We receive his word in faith, live in hope of its promise, and act on it in love.

What is the role of the Holy Spirit in communicating God's word to us?

Liturgy Link

The *Rite of Confirmation* states: "Great emphasis should be placed on the celebration of the word of God that introduces the rite of Confirmation. It is from the hearing of the word of God that the many-sided work of the Holy Spirit flows out upon the Church and upon each one of the baptized and confirmed. Through this hearing of his word God's will is made known in the life of Christians" (*Rite of Confirmation,* "Introduction" 13).

lifelinks

In a small group list three key things you have come to know about God from Sacred Scripture and from the teachings of the Church. Circle one and describe how it makes a difference for your life.

What I Have Come to Know	The Difference It Makes
_____	_____
_____	_____
_____	_____

The Liturgy of the Word

Ritual Focus

Why is the Liturgy of the Word an essential part of the celebration of Confirmation?

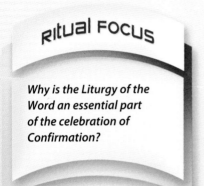
Faith vocabulary

Liturgy of the Word
The part of the Church's liturgical celebrations during which the Sacred Scriptures are proclaimed and the assembly of the faithful is invited to respond with faith.

Lectionary
The book that contains the Scripture readings that are assigned to be proclaimed at the celebration of the liturgy.

Digital forms of communication that have changed the way families, friends, and businesses carry on relationships each day. Yet, for all that is new about today's communication technologies, people still connect by communicating in words and actions that allow them to be present with one another. The **Liturgy of the Word** of the Word of God includes words and other ritual gestures and the assembly of the faithful's response in faith.

Roots in Ancient Jewish Worship

The Liturgy of the Word at Mass as we celebrate it today is rooted in ancient Jewish worship rituals. In both the Old Testament and the New Testament we read about the Jewish people not only gathering to listen to the proclamation of God's word but also responding to his word by renewing their commitment to live the Covenant. For example, Luke 4:16–20 describes a synagogue service at which Jesus gathered with the people of Nazareth for the proclamation of the Scriptures of ancient Israel. These synagogue services of the Word of God became the model for proclaiming the Word of God when the early Church gathered.

Today, the celebration of the Liturgy of the Word at Mass is similar to the ritual of the ancient Jewish people. God's word is solemnly spoken among the faithful, and he is present and acts with power in the assembly's midst. That is why we treat Sacred Scripture, the Word of God and the book in which it has been written down, with such respect and reverence.

Listening with Faith, Hope, and Love

The Lectionary is the book that contains the Scripture readings that are assigned to be proclaimed at the celebration of the liturgy. For the celebration of the Sacrament of Confirmation the Lectionary designates five Old Testament texts for the First Reading, six Psalms for the Responsorial Psalm, twelve New Testament texts for the Second Reading, and twelve Gospel selections for the Gospel Proclamation. In these Scripture passages God has revealed himself to be the mystery of One God in three divine Persons—God the Father, God the Son, and God the Holy Spirit. We call this mystery of One God in three divine Persons the mystery of the Holy, or Blessed, Trinity.

When Sacred Scripture is proclaimed during the Liturgy of the Word on the day of your Confirmation, how ready will you be to listen to what God is telling you about himself? How ready will you be to experience God's presence in word and deed on that day? How open will your heart be to respond in faith, hope, and love to God, who invites you to live in friendship and communion with him?

How ready will you be to open yourself to the Gifts of the Holy Spirit that he wants to pour out upon you that day? To be ready you must prepare yourself. The Church puts it this way, "[I]t is necessary that the faithful come to [the liturgy] with proper dispositions" (*Constitution on the Sacred Liturgy* 11).

Why is it important to participate fully in the Liturgy of the Word?

Liturgy Link

There are many actions the Church uses during the Liturgy of the Word to show reverence for God's word. We stand for the proclamation of the Gospel. The Book of the Gospels is often surrounded by lighted candles and is incensed before the priest or deacon proclaims the Gospel. After reading from the Gospel, the priest or deacon kisses the page where Jesus' words are contained. The assembly responds at the end of each reading with a special acclamation, acknowledging that they have listened to the Word of God.

lifelinks

Think about what you can do to prepare yourself to participate actively, fully, and consciously in the Liturgy of the Word at your Confirmation and at every liturgical celebration. List what you will do.

_____

_____

_____

The Church Lives the Faith

Faith-filled people who have listened to the Word of God, taken it to heart, and made it part of their lives continue to play a significant role in the history of the Church. Saint Anthony of the Desert is one example of such a faith-filled person. When he heard the Gospel passage "If you wish to be perfect, go, sell what you have and give to [the] poor . . . Then come, follow me" (Matthew 19:21), Saint Anthony responded by doing exactly that. He gave all his possessions to the poor and lived out the rest of his life as a person of prayer in solitude in the desert. Christians today respond to the Word of God and make similar heroic responses to the one made in the fourth century by Saint Anthony of the Desert. Sister Dorothy Stang is one of those heroic Christians.

Sister Dorothy Stang.

The Angel of Trans-Amazonia

Sister Dorothy Stang, a member of the Sisters of Notre Dame de Namur, worked for several decades with the rural poor of the Amazon rain forest basin in Brazil, South America. Because of her work of helping and advising the rural poor to protect their land, Sister Dorothy received numerous death threats from wealthy landowners and loggers who wished to profit by cutting down the trees in the rain forest. Despite these threats, Sister Dorothy continued to be outspoken in her efforts on behalf of both the poor and the environment.

Sister Dorothy visiting village in Amazon region.

A Witness for Christ

Sister Dorothy's ministry resulted in her giving her life for the people. According to news reports, two gunmen approached her on February 12, 2005, and aimed their weapons at her while she was reading the Bible. Witnesses reported that while at gunpoint, she read the Beatitude "Blessed are the peacemakers, / for they will be called children of God" (Matthew 5:9) to her assassins. The assailants, whom police said were hired by Brazilian landowners, responded by shooting her at point-blank range.

Funeral procession from airport to Santas Missoes Church in Anapu, Northern Brazil, February 14, 2005.

Sister Dorothy responded to the Word of God by reaching out to the rural poor of Brazil. That response included her standing on the side of the poor, no matter what. In the end, she proclaimed God's word, not only by the words she uttered from the Gospel, but just as loudly by her life of solidarity with "the least of my brothers" (Matthew 25:40). As news of her death spread, more than two thousand poor Brazilian farmers marched to the remote jungle town of Anapu for the funeral of this seventy-three-year-old woman whom they called the "Angel of Trans-Amazonia."

When has your response to the proclamation of the Word of God required you to act with courage to be a witness for Christ?

Procession to cemetery.

Living the Faith
Makes a Difference

We have all been with people at one time or another who seem not to pay much attention to us when we are trying to communicate with them. They are so distracted or distant that it seems as if they are not really "there"—beyond their mere physical presence to us. We have also known people who are so tuned in to what we are saying or doing that they quickly come to understand and respond. In other words, the latter group has good interpersonal communication skills.

Interpersonal Communication

Good interpersonal communication skills do not just come about by chance. People learn and develop these skills over a lifetime. One of the most basic of these skills is active listening.

Researchers tell us that while most people speak at a rate of between 100 and 175 words per minute, we can listen intelligently at a rate of 600 to 800 words per minute. Since only a part of our mind is required to follow a speaker, it is easy to let our minds drift while we are listening. The cure for this is active listening. Active listening is a skill which allows us to be intent and focused on the other person in a very deliberate way.

Developing Active-Listening Skills

Fortunately, a good bit of study has been devoted to the skills and qualities that go into making someone an active listener. Active listening includes being involved on a thinking and a feeling level both to the person speaking and to what is being said. Here are some tips to help you become a better active listener:

* **Be present.** Focus your attention deliberately on the person who is speaking and on what is being communicated. Avoid distractions.

* **Make eye contact.** Look directly at the person who is speaking. Listen not only with your ears but also with your eyes and other senses.

* **Be open-minded.** Avoid making quick judgments about what the person is saying.

* **Clarify.** Acknowledge and clarify points as they are being communicated.

* **Communicate.** Show interest in what is being said through verbal and nonverbal actions.

While you are learning how to more effectively listen and respond to God's word, it is also important to develop good listening skills and to become an active listener. Listening actively will help you grow as a member of the Body of Christ.

Faith Decision

• In a small group identify the things you have found that help you to be an active listener. Then discuss how you can strengthen these skills.

• Next, review your responses to the "Life Links" activity on page 19. Reflect on what can be done to overcome those obstacles.

• Finally, think about the steps you can personally take to become a better active and attentive listener.

This week I will listen more attentively to God's presence in my life by

_____

_____

_____.

my thoughts

In this chapter you reflected on the Liturgy of the Word that precedes the celebration of the rite of Confirmation. You have learned more about the significance of this part of the celebration of Confirmation. You have discussed the importance of listening attentively and responding to God's word by making it part of your daily life.

Write about the ways you can become a better "hearer of the word" as part of your preparation for the day of your Confirmation.

_____

_____

_____

_____

_____

_____

_____

_____

_____

_____

_____

A question to share with your sponsor and parents:

How have you encountered the Scriptures in the Liturgy of the Word, in reading the Bible individually, or in other ways that have "made a difference" in your life?

Renewing Baptismal Promises

Reflection on the Opening Ritual

What were you thinking and feeling as you signed yourself with the holy water during the opening ritual?

There are many things we routinely do each day. It can happen that we do these things without giving them much thought. Blessing ourselves as we pray the Sign of the Cross is such a simple prayer that we can easily forget all that it represents. When we pray the Sign of the Cross, we profess faith in the Blessed Trinity and in the death, Resurrection, and Ascension of Jesus Christ. We recall our Baptism through which we were joined to Christ and initiated into his Church.

How might we become more aware of the true significance of some of our most familiar rituals of the Church?

Disciples of Jesus

Faith vocabulary

Pharisee
A member of a Jewish sect in Jesus' time whose members dedicated their lives to the strict keeping of the Law found in the Torah.

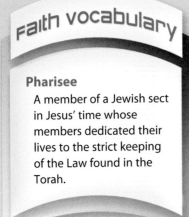

Detail from *Christ Driving Out Those Bought and Sold.* James J. Tissot (1836–1902), French painter.

When have you had to make an either-or choice or take sides on a controversial issue? Your saying yes to one side frequently means saying no to the other. This sometimes can be a very difficult choice. It can even be a life-changing choice.

Life-Changing Choices

John's Gospel contains many accounts of either-or choices. John speaks about choosing light or darkness, life or death, truth or falsehood, sight or blindness, faith or disbelief. John never misses an opportunity to remind his readers that being a loyal and faithful disciple of Jesus Christ demands making life-changing choices.

John's Gospel describes a conversation between Jesus and Nicodemus (John 3:1–21), a **Pharisee** who comes to Jesus secretly in the darkness of the night. This narrative reveals a great deal about the life-changing choice one must make for or against Jesus.

The scene in chapter 2 of John's Gospel just before the story of Nicodemus's conversation with Jesus provides the context for understanding the meaning of that conversation. It is Passover, and Jesus has come to Jerusalem for the feast and has just driven out the money changers from the Temple in Jerusalem, angering the Jewish leaders. No wonder Nicodemus was afraid of being seen with Jesus.

Living in the Light

This narrative about the conversation between Jesus and Nicodemus opens with the detail that Nicodemus comes to Jesus "at night" (John 3:2). While this seems to be a small detail, it is significant and symbolic, pointing to more than the physical darkness of the night. The nighttime suggests that Nicodemus is still a captive of the powers of darkness and not yet willing to declare himself openly as a disciple of Jesus, "the true light, which enlightens everyone" (John 1:9). We read:

> [Nicodemus] came to Jesus at night and said to him, "Rabbi, we know that you are a teacher who has come from God, . . ." Jesus answered and said to him, "Amen, amen, I say to you, no one can see the kingdom of God without being born from above." Nicodemus said to him, "How can a person once grown old be born again? . . ." Jesus answered, "Amen, amen, I say to you, no one can enter the kingdom of God without being born of water and Spirit."
>
> JOHN 3:1–5, 16

Detail from
Interview Between Jesus and Nicodemus. James J. Tissot.

While Nicodemus's response "How can a person once grown old be born again?" reveals that he still does not understand what Jesus is saying, the early Church would have immediately recognized these words as referring to Baptism. Jesus concludes by telling Nicodemus that choosing to be a disciple of Jesus includes choosing between light and darkness.

What does Jesus teach Nicodemus about the choice required of anyone who wishes to be his disciple?

lifelinks

Think about three choices that you had to make about being a witness for Christ. Identify what you were saying yes to and what you were saying no to. List your choices.

_____

_____

_____

The Paschal Mystery

Doctrine Focus

What is a person committing to when first making or renewing the baptismal promises?

Faith Vocabulary

Period of Purification and Enlightenment
The last stage of the catechumenal process in the rite of Christian Initiation, which coincides with the Season of Lent.

Paschal Mystery
The saving events of the Passion, death, Resurrection, and glorious Ascension of Jesus Christ.

When there are catechumens, or people who have not yet been baptized, in a parish preparing for initiation into the Church at the Easter Vigil, the Season of Lent is called the **Period of Purification and Enlightenment.** This stage of the initiation process is a time of final and intense spiritual preparation. It is a time when the entire Christian community is invited to join the catechumens in turning away from the darkness of sin (purification) and turning toward the light of Christ (enlightenment).

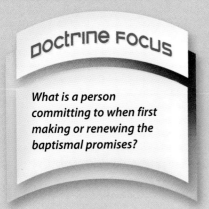

Rejecting Death and Choosing New Life

The Period of Purification and Enlightenment reflects the Gospel call to repent and believe in the Gospel. It mirrors the saving events of the **Paschal Mystery** of Christ, of Salvation from sin and rebirth in new life promised in Christ.

At the heart of the Gospel is the dynamic movement of conversion to Christ, of moving from death to life, of turning away from sin and turning toward Christ. From the very earliest centuries of the Church, the liturgy of Christian initiation has captured this twofold movement of turning from sin and turning toward Christ in the form of making promises to reject Satan and his works and to live as children of the light.

In denouncing the works of Satan, the catechumens promise to reject and not take part in acts of darkness which, among other things, include acts of racism, ethnic hatred, or bigotry. They promise to reject and give up all forms of violence, from schoolyard bullying to unjust warfare. They forsake all excessive and inappropriate desire for power, wealth, success, and pleasure. When those about to be baptized promise to reject the works of Satan, they are really pledging to embrace a life of ongoing conversion to Christ. In so doing, they are making the life-changing promise to live according to the Gospel as witnesses for Christ.

Confessing that Jesus Is Lord

In the baptismal promises which you will renew as part of the rite of Confirmation, you solemnly reject all that Satan stands for and commit yourself to doing the works of God. The New Testament Book of Revelation describes in graphic and lurid imagery the works of Satan as blasphemy, violence, misuse of authority, and the perversion of all that Christ represents. The Book of Revelation also announces that in the Resurrection of Jesus, the victory over those powers of darkness has already been won.

The origin of the Apostles Creed is found in the baptismal profession of faith in the Holy Trinity—in One God in three Persons, God the Father, God the Son, and God the Holy Spirit—and in the Trinity's works of creation, salvation, and sanctification. Those who wish to be disciples of Jesus Christ must publicly profess their faith in the Holy Trinity and affirm that Jesus and he alone is Lord, the Victor over sin and over death itself.

Saint Paul wrote to the Church in Rome, "[I]f you confess with your mouth that Jesus is Lord and believe in your heart that God raised him from the dead, you will be saved" (Romans 10:9). When the bishop asks you to renew your baptismal promises before you are confirmed, you are being invited to choose Jesus, the Light of the world, and all that he stands for over darkness, just as Jesus invited Nicodemus to do.

What is the connection between the Paschal Mystery and the baptismal promises?

Liturgy Link

A candidate for Confirmation who has attained the age of reason must profess faith, be in the state of grace, have the intention of receiving the sacrament, and be prepared to assume the role of disciple and witness to Christ, both within the Church and in the world. A candidate should receive the Sacrament of Penance to prepare oneself to receive the strength and grace of the Holy Spirit. (See *Catechism of the Catholic Church* 1310, 1318, and 1319.)

lifelinks

Make a list of the behaviors that describe a person who turns away from the works of Satan and toward Christ. Which of these behaviors describes you?

_____

_____

_____

A Solemn Commitment

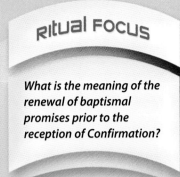

Ritual Focus

What is the meaning of the renewal of baptismal promises prior to the reception of Confirmation?

Faith Vocabulary

Viaticum

The name given to Holy Communion when it is administered to a dying person as food and strength for their journey from life on earth, through death, to eternal life.

When people join an organization, there are often rituals involved that include the use of symbols. This helps people understand the nature of the group they are joining and their responsibilities as members of the group. The Church too uses many symbols and rituals in the celebration of the sacraments.

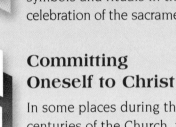

Committing Oneself to Christ

In some places during the early centuries of the Church, those to be baptized had to face toward the west—the realm of darkness where

Baptism by immersion.

the sun set. Then they three times rejected sin, evil, and Satan with all his lies and temptations. They even sometimes had to spit toward the darkness, showing their complete contempt for all forms of wickedness.

After this threefold rejection of Satan and his works, a threefold profession of the faith of the Church was made by those about to be baptized. For this profession of faith, the candidates turned toward the east—the direction from which the sun rises, bringing with it the light. Stepping into the baptismal pool, they were first asked to profess faith in God the Father and Creator and were then plunged, or immersed, completely underwater as the celebrant prayed, "(*Name*), I baptize you in the name of the Father, and of the Son, and of the Holy Spirit." Next, they professed faith in Jesus Christ, and were once again completely immersed underwater. Then they professed faith in the Holy Spirit, followed by their third and final immersion into the water.

Everyone witnessing a Baptism knew without a doubt that those being baptized were committing themselves to be faithful followers of Jesus Christ. They had sworn an oath, a *sacramentum*, in a highly public manner. Christians borrowed the Latin term *sacramentum*, which originally referred to the oath that Roman soldiers took, binding themselves for life to the service of the Emperor, and gave it a new meaning. Christians swore an oath to be bound for life to serve Jesus alone as Lord. The *Rite of Confirmation* states that candidates to be confirmed "must be . . . properly instructed, and capable of renewing the baptismal promises" ("Introduction," *Rite of Confirmation* 12). Understanding the many ways the Catholic Church includes the renewal of baptismal promises in the liturgy can help us grasp the significance of this practice of the Church.

Looking at the ritual prescribed for a dying person gives us some inkling of how solemn a moment it is when a baptized person publicly renews their commitment to live and die as followers of Jesus Christ. In that ritual the priest is directed to have the person renew their baptismal promises before receiving **Viaticum.** Viaticum is the name given to Holy Communion when it is administered to a dying person as food and strength for their journey from life on earth, through death, to eternal life.

Imagine how seriously you would take this part of the rite of Confirmation if you knew that shortly afterward you would be facing death. That, in fact, is not too far removed from the awareness that must have been present in the early Church for those initiated at the Easter Vigil. They knew that, at any time, persecution by the Roman Emperor could easily mean death for them.

What does the baptismal ritual of the threefold rejection and threefold profession symbolize?

LiTURGY LiNK

In the early centuries of the Church, Baptism and Confirmation were always celebrated together. What was begun in Baptism is strengthened in Confirmation. The link between these two Sacraments of Christian Initiation is very close. This is why when a baptized person celebrates Confirmation separated in time from their celebration of Baptism, the renewal of baptismal promises is part of the rite.

lifelinks

In a small group discuss why the renewal of baptismal promises is such a solemn moment in the rite of Confirmation. Then discuss what candidates must be "capable of" in order to renew their baptismal promises. Use this space to record the key ideas of your group's discussion.

_____

_____

_____

The Church
Lives the Faith

One of the most significant results of the Second Vatican Council was the Church's renewed focus on the role and dignity of laypeople. Increasingly, laypeople came to realize that their mission as baptized and confirmed disciples is to work to transform the world from within so that God's reign might more fully and swiftly come to its fulfillment. The realization of what it means to be a Christian lay-disciple of Christ has manifested itself in an incredible growth in the number of laypeople involved in ministries of various kinds. One of those ministries is the Jesuit Volunteer Corps (JVC).

The Jesuit Volunteer Corps

Since its founding shortly before the Second Vatican Council began in 1962, more than 12,000 lay men and women have participated in the Jesuit Volunteer Corps. After graduating from college, young men and women make a commitment to work among the poor for one year or more as part of the JVC network. Volunteers serve the homeless, the unemployed, refugees, people with AIDS, the elderly, street youth, abused women and children, the mentally ill, and the developmentally disabled.

The Jesuit Volunteer Corps has become the largest Catholic lay volunteer program in the United States of America. JVC members live out their commitment in a variety of ways that integrate the values of social justice, simplicity of lifestyle, community living, and spirituality.

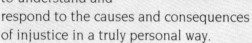

▼ **Social justice:** Social justice is a lived experience as JVC members form person-to-person relationships with the poor. This enables JVC members to understand and respond to the causes and consequences of injustice in a truly personal way.

▼ **Simple lifestyle:** Living a simple lifestyle frees volunteers to experience the value of simple pleasures. Volunteers shape their common lifestyle by making group decisions about food purchases, recycling, appliance usage, and so on.

▼ **Community living:** JVC members live together in group households that provide a dependable way of giving and receiving support. By sharing dinner, discussions, prayer, and leisure activities, JVC members renew and encourage one another to continue their ministries.

▼ **Spirituality:** Spirituality for the JVC member is focused on being a "contemplative in action," that is, working actively for and with the poor, and reflecting on God's presence in work and relationships. JVC spirituality is based on the spirituality of Saint Ignatius Loyola (1491–1556), the founder of the Jesuits.

If you would like to find out more about the Jesuit Volunteer Corps, you can check out their Web site at www.jesuitvolunteers.org.

How is the Jesuit Volunteer Corps an example of Christians who have discovered the deeper meaning of their Baptism and Confirmation?

Living the Faith
Makes a Difference

The *Catechism of the Catholic Church* teaches that we first receive the Gifts of the Holy Spirit in Baptism (1266) and that in Confirmation these gifts are increased within us (1303). In the rite of Confirmation the bishop specifically names courage as one of the seven Gifts of the Holy Spirit as he prays with his hands extended over you.

The Gift of Courage

People often report that they acted heroically not in an absence of fear, but in spite of being afraid. Mark Twain said, "Courage is resistance to fear, mastery of fear—not absence of fear." Courage is the inner strength that allows us to conquer the fear of being witnesses for Christ and do the right thing, no matter what the cost.

Each of us has certain things we are afraid of. Some common fears that people have include fear of public speaking, fear of heights, fear of water, and fear of darkness, just to name a few. For some people fear can be paralyzing. Fears can hold us back from being the people we were created to be. For other people fears can become the source of energy to accomplish positive goals. For example, fear of failure can energize a student to study more diligently.

We can work at overcoming and using our fears to achieve positive goals by looking them squarely in the face, understanding where they come from, and discovering what it is about them that we find so terrifying. Remember, courage is not the absence of fear; it is mastering our fears and learning how to act in the face of fear.

Faith Decision

Use this chart to examine the role that fear plays in your life and to identify positive steps you can take to overcome some of those fears. One example has been given to get you started.

Name of the fear (add others as a result of your discussion)	What it is that is underneath this fear (what you are really afraid of)	Name the strength of this fear for you (1 = not at all; 10 = overwhelming, paralyzing fear)	Identify steps you would like to take to overcome the effects of this fear in your life
Challenging my best friend's behavior in a certain matter	Losing my best friend; being teased because I said something	7	Get advice from school counselor on how to confront without alienating

This week I will pray about and challenge one of the fears that is an obstacle to my living as a disciple of Jesus. To overcome that fear I will

_____

_____

_____ .

my thoughts

In this chapter you explored the renewal of baptismal promises, which is part of the celebration of the rite of Confirmation. You learned about the significance of this ritual and how it invites you to make a very deliberate choice to be a disciple of Jesus Christ. You live out that choice every day and every week in a variety of ways—with family and friends, at school, and in social situations.

In your journal write your thoughts about how you can more actively and consistently choose to be a disciple of Jesus Christ in your day-to-day life.

_____

_____

_____

_____

_____

_____

_____

_____

_____

_____

_____

_____

_____

A question to share with your sponsor and parents:

What have you learned from your experiences about how to make choices to live as a disciple of Christ?

Chapter 4

Laying On of Hands

Reflection on the Opening Ritual

What was your experience as you received the laying on of hands and the prayer of blessing in the opening ritual?

In many ethnic groups there is a tradition of parents placing their hand on their children's heads each night at bedtime as a sign and prayer of blessing. A remnant of this custom still survives in its secular form when an adult pats a child on the head as a gesture of good will.

What are some examples in the Bible in which someone uses touch or the laying on of hands to symbolize God's action in another person's life?

Baptism (top),
Confirmation candidate
and sponsor (bottom).

Receiving the Holy Spirit

Scripture Focus

What are some of the meanings associated with the action of laying on of hands in the Bible?

Faith vocabulary

scapegoat
A term that refers to an individual who carries the blame or guilt of others; originally an animal on whom the Jewish High Priest laid hands in a ritual ceremony, transferring the guilt of the Israelite people, and then banishing the animal to the desert so that it would "carry away" the people's sins.

The body language of people—the way they look, the way they use their hands, the tone of their voice—often communicates more than their words. Sacred Scripture contains numerous examples of the use of hands as a way of communicating the mystery of God at work in the lives of his people.

Old Testament

In the opening ritual we listened to Genesis 48:13–16 in which a blessing was conferred on Ephraim and Manasseh by Jacob with a laying on of hands. The Old Testament contains other examples and uses of the laying on of hands. Two of these uses are the practice of scapegoating and the commissioning of a person for service to God's people.

The term **scapegoat** refers to an individual who carries the blame or guilt of others. The Israelites adopted the term and practice and used it in their worship. This practice is described in Leviticus 16:20–22.

The laying on of hands is also used in the Old Testament to convey a transfer of power with a commissioning for a specific office or mission. This use of laying on of hands is found in the Book of Numbers. We read:

> And the Lord replied to Moses, "Take Joshua, son of Nun, a man of spirit, and lay your hand upon him. Have him stand in the presence of the priest Eleazar and of the whole community, and commission him before their eyes, . . . that the whole Israelite community may obey him."
>
> NUMBERS 27:18–20

Detail from *Moses Blesseth Josuah Before the High Priests.* James J. Tissot (1836–1902), French painter.

New Testament

The early Church adopted and gave the ritual of laying on of hands specifically Christian meanings. Two of the meanings given to this ritual gesture are "invoking the Holy Spirit" and "commissioning to office."

Invoking the Holy Spirit. After the event of Pentecost, the first disciples began to suffer persecution in and around Jerusalem. As a result many disciples fled to Samaria to fulfill Christ's command to make disciples of all people. The Apostles Peter and John were called there to lay their hands on those who only had been baptized. Luke tells us "they laid hands on them and they received the holy Spirit" (Acts of the Apostles 8:17).

Commissioning to Office. Saint Timothy was both a disciple and sometime companion to Saint Paul. The Second Letter to Timothy describes the final days of Saint Paul and addresses the need for Timothy to continue the work of Paul through the power of the Holy Spirit. In the opening of this letter we read:

> For this reason, I remind you to stir into flame the gift of God that you have through the imposition of my hands.   2 TIMOTHY 1:6

In both the Old Testament and New Testament the gesture of the laying on of hands has a variety of meanings. In each of these contexts, however, it is the Holy Spirit that is at work.

What are some of the meanings found in Sacred Scripture of the ritual of laying on of hands?

Saint Timothy (left) and Saint Paul the Apostle (right) laying hands on the baptized, stained glass.

lifelinks

Recall some of the special loving actions through which your family members reveal their love for you. Describe how these actions help you understand something of the mystery of God's love for you. Write your thoughts in this space or in your journal.

_____

_____

_____

Invoking the Holy Spirit

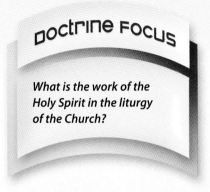

Doctrine Focus

What is the work of the Holy Spirit in the liturgy of the Church?

Faith Vocabulary

epiclesis
The name given to the prayer that invokes the transforming presence of the Holy Spirit.

Saint Paul the Apostle, to whom the majority of the New Testament Letters are attributed, clarifies the early Church's understanding of the work of the Holy Spirit over and over again. This is the Holy Spirit that will be poured out on you at your Confirmation and strengthen you to live your Baptism.

The Works of the Holy Spirit in the Liturgy

In his letter to the Church in Rome, Saint Paul specifically teaches about the work of the Holy Spirit in the Church's worship. He writes that it is the love of God "poured out into our hearts through the holy Spirit" (Romans 5:5) who teaches us how to pray.

The Church today speaks to this tradition and identifies four key roles that the Holy Spirit plays in the liturgy. They are:

- to prepare the assembly to encounter Christ;
- to recall and manifest Christ to the assembly;
- to make the saving work of Christ present and active by his transforming power; and
- to bring us into communion with Christ and so to form his Body (*Catechism of the Catholic Church* 1093–1112).

In the celebration of each of the sacraments, the Church calls upon God the Father to send down his Holy Spirit to transform us more and more into the Body of Christ. We name this prayer of invoking, or calling down, the Holy Spirit's transforming power the **epiclesis.**

Transformed by the Holy Spirit

We are most familiar with an epiclesis from the Eucharistic Prayer. Prior to the words of consecration, the priest extends his hands over the bread and wine and prays:

Father, we bring you these gifts.
We ask you to make them holy by the power
    of your Spirit,
that they may become the body and blood
of your Son, our Lord Jesus Christ,
at whose command we celebrate this eucharist.

EUCHARISTIC PRAYER III

The hushed prayerfulness of the epiclesis is a very solemn moment in the Eucharistic liturgy. Then the priest takes the bread and wine and speaks the words of institution, or words of consecration, spoken by Jesus at the Last Supper. Through the power of the Holy Spirit and words of the priest, the bread and wine become the Body and Blood of Christ.

At your Confirmation the bishop and the priest celebrating with him will extend their hands over you and the other candidates as they pray that you might be strengthened with the seven Gifts of the Holy Spirit. As the bishop extends his hands over you and prays the epiclesis at your Confirmation, a moment of great solemnity has arrived. The Church prays that through the power of the Holy Spirit your life in Christ will be a living sacrifice to God, that you will be transformed more deeply into the image of Christ, that you will grow in love for the Church, and that you will participate in the Church's mission through the witness and service of love.

What happens during the epiclesis in the rite of Confirmation?

Liturgy Link

There is a second epiclesis prayed during the celebration of the Eucharist. It occurs when the priest asks the Holy Spirit to transform the faithful who are assembled so that they may become one with Christ.

lifelinks

Work in small groups to look up and read these passages from the Old Testament: Ezekiel 36:22–28, Ezekiel 37:1–14, and Joel 3:1–5. As you read each passage imagine the prophet is speaking to you. Describe how reading these passages helps you prepare for Confirmation.

_____

_____

_____

The Gifts of the Holy Spirit

Faith vocabulary

Messiah
The Hebrew word *messiah* is translated into Greek as *christos* (Christ) and means "anointed one"; the Anointed One whom God promised to send his people to save them.

Sometimes the full meaning of certain gestures is only grasped by listening to and reflecting on the words that accompany them. For example, how does a teacher know whether we want to ask a question or be excused for a moment when we raise our hand in class? It is only by listening to the words that are used with the gesture of raising our hand.

The Pouring Out of the Holy Spirit

In the rite of Confirmation the words of the bishop's prayer as he extends his hands over the candidates reveal the meaning of this familiar gesture. The use of the prayer invoking the Holy Spirit can be traced at least to the sixth and perhaps even the fourth century. The origins of its meaning can be found in Isaiah 11:2, where the prophet promises that YHWH (the letters of the name God used to reveal himself to Moses) would send the Jewish people a deliverer, an anointed one, in Hebrew, a **messiah.** We read:

> The spirit of the Lord shall rest upon him:
>> a spirit of wisdom and of understanding,
> A spirit of counsel and of strength,
>> a spirit of knowledge and of fear of the Lord.
>
> ISAIAH 11:2

This and other similar texts of the prophets came to be known collectively as messianic prophecies. Over many centuries these passages sustained the hope of the Jewish people during times of adversity. The promise of a spirit from YHWH being poured out on a chosen, anointed one grew in importance throughout Jewish history. At the time of Jesus the hope for and expectation of the coming of this messiah was great. Jesus announced in the synagogue at Nazareth (Luke 4:16–20) that he was the One promised by YHWH.

Laying on of hands during the celebration of the Sacrament of Confirmation.

The Holy Spirit, Helper and Guide

After you have renewed your baptismal promises in the rite of Confirmation, the bishop will extend his hands over you, linking you to this long history of individuals chosen by God. The bishop will ask the entire assembly to pray with him that you will be given the gift of the Holy Spirit and that you will be anointed to be more like Christ.

The bishop's prayer first asks for the Holy Spirit to be sent upon you as Helper and Guide, and then requests that you be given the sevenfold Gifts of the Holy Spirit. He prays:

All-powerful God, Father of our Lord Jesus Christ, . . .
Give them the spirit of wisdom and understanding,
the spirit of right judgment and courage,
the spirit of knowledge and reverence.
Fill them with the spirit of wonder and awe
     in your presence.

There is really only one gift, the Holy Spirit himself, who makes his presence felt in your life at different levels and in different areas of activity by means of the seven gifts named in the prayer: wisdom, understanding, right judgment, courage, knowledge, reverence, and wonder and awe.

What the bishop and the community are praying for is that the Holy Spirit who empowered Jesus for his mission and accompanied him to do the works the Father sent him to do may also be in and with those whom the Church confirms. By sharing in that same Holy Spirit, those who are confirmed share in Jesus' mission as well.

What does the laying on of hands in the rite of Confirmation tell about the role of the Holy Spirit in your life?

lifelinks

List the times you have witnessed the laying on of hands during the celebration of the sacraments. Compare your understanding of the use of that action then and your understanding now.

Experience	Then	Now
_____	_____	_____
_____	_____	_____
_____	_____	_____

The Church
Lives the Faith

On several occasions, the Gospels describe Jesus touching people and healing them. One example is his healing of a leper who asked him for a cure. (See Matthew 8:1–4.) This was an unexpected action of Jesus that would have startled those who witnessed it. Why is that? Jewish law banned those who suffered from this condition from contact with the rest of the community. Any contact with such a person rendered someone impure and unable to take part in Jewish worship. But that is exactly what Jesus did, and he made it clear that he expected his disciples to go out and do likewise. (See Matthew 10:8.) Blessed Damien of Molokai took Jesus' command seriously.

Father Damien (1840–1889) with choir, Molokai, Hawaii.

Blessed Damien of Molokai

Damien was born on January 3, 1840, in Tremeloo, Belgium, and was baptized with the name Joseph. Following the example of his older brother, he joined the Congregation of the Sacred Hearts of Jesus and Mary, took the religious name Damien, and studied for the priesthood. In 1864 he was sent to Hawaii where he was ordained a priest and served the native peoples of Hawaii as a missionary.

After nearly ten years working as a missionary, Damien convinced his religious superiors to send him to the island of Molokai, where people suffering from leprosy had been sent to live segregated from the rest of the population. Just as in Jesus' time, they were made to be social outcasts and judged by many to have been punished for leading sinful lives.

Damien soon experienced for himself the emotional loneliness and sadness that accompanied the physical illnesses and suffering of the outcasts on Molokai. This led Damien to see their need to be touched, both physically and spiritually, so he reached out to them without fear for his personal safety.

Father Damien eventually contracted the disease himself in the early 1880s and continued to care for others in the midst of his own suffering. After twenty-five years in Hawaii, Father Damien died from the effects of leprosy on April 15, 1889. On June 4, 1995, he was declared Blessed of the Church by Pope John Paul II.

Who do you know or who have you read about who has reached out and touched the lives of people who have been cast out by their friends, neighbors, or community? Work with a partner and share what you know about these people.

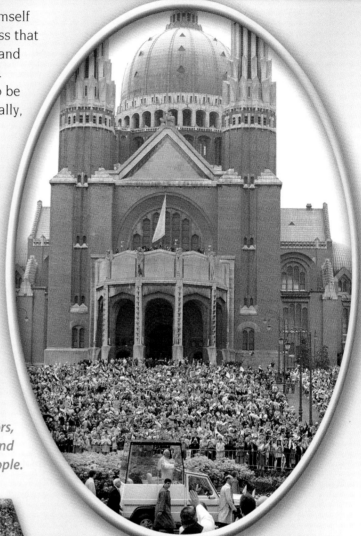

Pope John Paul II at beatification of Father Damian, Basilica of Koekelberg in Brussels, Belgium, June 4, 1995.

JOSEPH DAMIEN DE VEUSTER, BORN 3RD JANUARY 1840, DIED 8TH APRIL 1889.

JOSEPH DAMIEN DE VEUSTER, HANAU I KA LA 3 O IANUALE 1840 MAKE I KA LA 8 O APELILA 1889

Memorial with inscription in English and Hawaiian, Tahitian, in Kalaupapa Village, Molokai.

Living the Faith
Makes a Difference

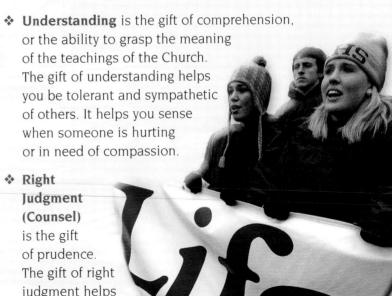

Look back to page 46 and reread Isaiah 11:2. What you will read is that the seven Gifts of the Holy Spirit were first mentioned nearly 3,000 years ago in the Book of Isaiah. The early Church initially took up that passage as a description of Jesus but eventually came to understand that it applies to all who are "anointed," that is, to every Christian who is "born of water and Spirit" (John 3:5).

Responding to the Gift of the Holy Spirit

As a candidate for the Sacrament of Confirmation, you are challenged to take this ancient heritage and make it part of your life today as a twenty-first-century Christian. These descriptions of the seven Gifts of the Holy Spirit can help you:

❖ **Wisdom** is the gift of knowing the right choices to make to live a holy life. The gift of wisdom helps you avoid the things that could lead you away from God.

❖ **Understanding** is the gift of comprehension, or the ability to grasp the meaning of the teachings of the Church. The gift of understanding helps you be tolerant and sympathetic of others. It helps you sense when someone is hurting or in need of compassion.

❖ **Right Judgment (Counsel)** is the gift of prudence. The gift of right judgment helps you make choices to live as a faithful follower of Jesus.

- ❖ **Courage (Fortitude)** is the gift that helps you stand up for your faith in Christ. The gift of courage helps you overcome any obstacles that would keep you from practicing your faith.

- ❖ **Knowledge** is the gift of knowing and enlightenment. The gift of knowledge enables you to choose the right path that will lead you to God. It encourages you to avoid obstacles that will keep you from him.

- ❖ **Reverence (Piety)** is the gift of confidence in God. This gift of reverence inspires you to joyfully want to serve God and others.

- ❖ **Wonder and Awe (Fear of the Lord)** is the gift of respect that encourages you to be in awe of God. The gift of wonder and awe moves you to so love God that you do not want to offend him by your words or actions.

Faith Decision

For each of the seven Gifts of the Holy Spirit, describe a practical example of what that gift would look like in your life.

_____
_____
_____
_____
_____

This week I will work to make the Gifts of the Holy Spirit a deeper part of my life. I will

_____
_____
_____ .

my thoughts

In this chapter you explored the biblical and Church traditions of the laying on of hands. You have learned about the significance of this ritual and how it calls down the Holy Spirit upon you. The process of your being transformed by the power of the Holy Spirit has already begun in your Baptism and has been ongoing through the regular reception of the Eucharist.

Write your thoughts about how you hope the Holy Spirit will further transform your life as a result of your Confirmation.

_____

_____

_____

_____

_____

_____

_____

_____

_____

_____

_____

_____

A question to share with your sponsor and parents:

How have the Gifts of the Holy Spirit strengthened you to be a witness for Christ?

chapter 5

Anointing with Chrism

Reflection on the Opening Ritual

Describe your experience as your forehead was anointed in the opening ritual.

All of us have probably used lotions or oils to protect or soothe our skin at one time or another. Parents rub baby oil on newborns after bathing them. Athletes are often given therapeutic massages with healing oils and other ointments. The Church rubs oil on, or anoints, people's hands, feet, and head in the celebration of the sacraments.

Think of a time when you have experienced the beneficial effects of oil or ointment. When have you witnessed oils being used during the celebration of the sacraments?

Chrism on table in front of stained-glass image of Holy Spirit.

God's Anointed Servant

scripture Focus

How was Jesus' anointing with the Holy Spirit like the anointing of Isaiah's Servant?

Faith vocabulary

Servant poems
A series of passages in the Book of Isaiah that describe the sufferings of the Servant of YHWH who will redeem God's people.

prefigure
A word meaning "to figure, or image, or announce beforehand."

At some point in your life, you have probably heard a friend or family member tell a story about something that happened to them. Their story may have been similar to an experience that you have had. Christians often better understand how God works in our lives by reading passages in the Bible. When we read or listen to Sacred Scripture, we often recognize that what is being described in a passage is similar to a life experience of our own.

Jesus' Mission Prefigured

Luke 4:16–22 describes Jesus standing up in the synagogue in Nazareth, reading a passage from the Book of Isaiah, and proclaiming that the Spirit of God was at work in his life. The text that Jesus read, Isaiah 61:1–2, is from a passage that speaks of God's activity in the world restoring God's people.

Baptism of Jesus, stained glass.

In Luke's account of the baptism of Jesus, which precedes the synagogue account, we read:

> After all the people had been baptized and Jesus also had been baptized and was praying, heaven opened and the holy Spirit descended upon him in bodily form like a dove. And a voice came from heaven, "You are my beloved Son; with you I am well pleased." LUKE 3:21–23

This identification of Jesus as God's "beloved Son" is the same description used in Isaiah 42:1, a passage that comes from one of the **Servant poems** in the Book of Isaiah. The Servant poems are a series of passages that describe the suffering Servant of God whose suffering will redeem God's people.

The early Church recognized the significance of Jesus' anointing with the Spirit at his baptism. Saint Peter, for example, said to the pagan Cornelius, "[You know] how God anointed Jesus of Nazareth with the holy Spirit and power. He went about doing good and healing all those oppressed by the devil, for God was with him" (Acts of the Apostles 10:38).

Jesus Christ, the Anointed One

The Servant in Isaiah's Servant poems is never clearly identified by the prophet. Some scholars think the Book of Isaiah had a specific historical figure in mind. Other scholars think the Servant was a figure representing the entire nation of Israel. The Church, under the guidance of the Holy Spirit, has come to recognize that this suffering Servant **prefigured,** or pointed to, Jesus of Nazareth, the Christ, the Anointed One.

In several verses after the passage from the Book of Isaiah that Jesus read in the synagogue, the prophet addresses the Jewish people. He uses words that we Christians can apply to ourselves. He says:

> You yourselves shall be named priests of the LORD,
>   ministers of our God you shall be called.
> Their descendants shall be renowned among
>   the nations, . . .
> All who see them shall acknowledge them
>   as a race the Lord has blessed. ISAIAH 61:6, 8, 9

We are "anointed ones" who share in the mission and ministry of Jesus Christ, Priest, Prophet, and King. The Church is "a chosen race, a royal priesthood, a holy nation, a people of [God's] own" (1 Peter 2:9).

What do we learn about Christ and the Church from the Book of Isaiah?

LITURGY LINK

Immediately after their Baptism, the newly baptized are anointed on the crown of their head with Chrism as the celebrant says, "The God of power and Father of our Lord Jesus Christ / has freed you from sin / brought you to new life / through water and the Holy Spirit. / He now anoints you with the chrism of salvation, / so that united with his people, / you may remain forever a member of Christ / who is Priest, Prophet, and King" (*Rite of Baptism* 62).

lifelinks

In a small group read Ephesians 1:1–14. Discuss how this passage helps you prepare for Confirmation and assume the responsibilities that flow from receiving this sacrament. Write your thoughts here.

_____

_____

_____

Consecrated for Mission

DOCTRINE FOCUS

What is the meaning of anointing with Chrism in the liturgy of the Church?

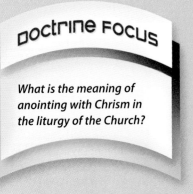

FAITH VOCABULARY

Chrism
Perfumed olive oil; one of the three oils blessed by the Church that is used in the celebration of Baptism, Confirmation, and Holy Orders, as well as in the consecration of churches, the altar, and sacred vessels.

The word *anoint* has several meanings, including "to smear or rub with oil," "to apply oil as a sacred rite, especially for consecration," and "to choose by or as if by divine election." The ritual anointing in the sacraments of the Church includes all of these meanings as it points to the mystery of God working in the Church and within the baptized.

The Mission of God's Anointed Ones

In the biblical tradition the actual physical application of oil, anointing, often represents that a thing or a person is being set aside, or consecrated, for a sacred use or a divine mission. Vessels used for worship were anointed with oil. So were kings in Israel. (See 1 Samuel 16:13.)

The Old Testament reveals that the connection between anointing and being given a share in the life of the Spirit of God was a key truth of faith among the Jewish people. This connection existed even when there was no physical use of oil. For example, the First Book of Kings tells us that after God told Elijah the Prophet to anoint Elisha (1 Kings 19:16), Elijah did not use oil; he did nothing more than "[throw] his cloak over him" (1 Kings 19:19).

This and other Old Testament passages help us understand how receiving the gift of the Holy Spirit came to be referred to as an anointing, especially when it was connected to God entrusting someone with a special mission.

The title *Christ* means "Anointed One" or "Messiah." The New Testament identifies Jesus as the Christ over 475 times. This attests to the Church's faith that Jesus is the Anointed One and Messiah. He is the One sent by his Father and anointed by the Holy Spirit to fulfill the mission of redeeming humankind.

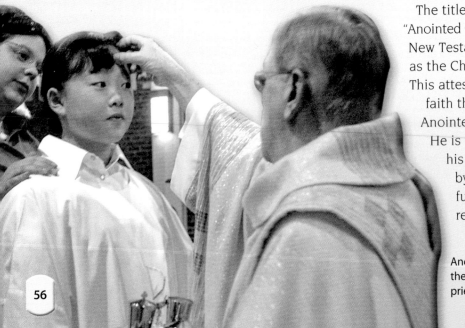

Anointing with Chrism during the rite of Confirmation by priest delegated by bishop.

Sharing in the Mission of Christ

Christians bear the name of Christ. Joined to Christ in Baptism we are reborn of water and the Holy Spirit, and in Confirmation we are sealed with the gift of the Holy Spirit. We are made sharers in the gift of Salvation and receive the responsibility to share that gift with others by participating in the mission of Jesus Christ in the world.

The gift of Salvation is the gift of divine forgiveness that has reconciled us with God. (See 2 Corinthians 5:18–19.) This wonderful gift, however, is given to us with a divine purpose: God the Father has chosen us to share in the mission of his Son. The anointing with the perfumed oil of **Chrism** in Baptism is a joyful expression of the fact that we are one with Jesus Christ. We are members of his body through whom he continues to live and act in the world, offering Salvation to one and all.

On the day of your Confirmation you will again be anointed with Chrism. The gift of the Holy Spirit you first received at Baptism and who chooses you and empowers you for such an astounding mission is renewed and strengthened.

Anointing crown of the head of a newly baptized infant.

What is the gift and mission you have received as a Christian, an "anointed one"?

Liturgy Link

Saint Cyril, a bishop of Jerusalem in the fourth century, preached a series of homilies during Easter week. Here is what he said to the neophytes, or those newly initiated into the Church, about their being anointed with sacred Chrism: "[S]ince you share in Christ it is right to call you Christs or anointed ones" (Mystagogical Catecheses 3).

lifelinks

Work in small groups and look through the four Gospels for times when Jesus explained his mission on earth. Discuss what Catholic teens do that shows they share in and continue Christ's work. Write your thoughts here.

_____

_____

_____

Called by Name

What is the significance of the anointing with Chrism in the rite of Confirmation?

Faith Vocabulary

Chrism Mass
The Mass celebrated during Holy Week, if possible on Holy Thursday morning, by the bishop of a diocese who consecrates the sacred Chrism and other oils that will be used at liturgies in every church of the diocese throughout the year.

Anointing of forehead with Chrism by bishop during the rite of Confirmation.

At the Second Vatican Council (1962–1965) the bishops taught that "the liturgy is made up of unchangeable elements divinely instituted, and of elements subject to change" (*Constitution on the Sacred Liturgy* 21). Although the essentials of our sacraments do not change over time, the outward form of those rituals has evolved throughout the history of the Church.

Sealed with the Gift of the Holy Spirit

Across the centuries the Church has made changes in the way that the rite of Confirmation is celebrated. In the first 500 years of the Church, a person was initiated into the Church through a process of evangelization and catechesis. This process of initiation involved a number of different ritual celebrations. The culmination of that process always led to a water rite (Baptism), the laying on of hands with anointing (Confirmation), and participation in the Lord's Supper (Eucharist) celebrated at the same time.

Today, the Churches of the East continue the practice of fully initiating a person (even infants) into the Church with all three rites in the same celebration. In the Church in the West, the celebration of the Sacrament of Confirmation was gradually separated from the celebration of the other two Sacraments of Christian Initiation, Baptism and Eucharist.

While under exceptional circumstances bishops sometimes delegated to priests the authority to confer Confirmation, they always reserved to themselves the consecration of the Chrism. Today, during Holy Week at the **Chrism Mass** on Holy Thursday morning, the bishop consecrates all the Chrism that will be used in the diocese throughout the year.

Immediately after the bishop has extended his hands and prayed over all the candidates, each of those to be confirmed approaches him individually. The sponsor accompanies the candidate and places their hand on the candidate's right shoulder. The bishop addresses each candidate by name. This underlines that this moment represents a very personal call from God calling the candidate by name to be anointed. Although the custom of taking a new saint's name as one's patron saint may still be observed, many see a value in using one's baptismal name as a way of showing the connection between Baptism and Confirmation.

The most solemn moment in the celebration now takes place. The words and actions essential to the sacrament now occur. As the bishop places his hand on top of your head, he anoints your forehead with Chrism, as he makes the sign of the cross, saying, "(N*ame*), be sealed with the gift of the Holy Spirit."

It is significant that the rite calls for you to respond, "Amen." You are not a passive recipient of the sacrament. You are an active partner as God calls you to discipleship on a still deeper level. Your "Amen" is a public "So be it!" It is your public acknowledgment and acceptance of what has just been celebrated.

What are you acknowledging when you respond "Amen" to your anointing in Confirmation?

Liturgy Link

In 1971 Pope Paul VI changed the words of the sacramental formula spoken by the bishop in the Sacrament of Confirmation. Previously, using a formula that can be traced back to the twelfth century, the bishop said, "I sign you with the sign of the cross and confirm you with the chrism of salvation, in the name of the Father . . ." The new formula of Pope Paul VI, "Be sealed with the gift of the Holy Spirit," is actually a very ancient one. Its use can be traced back as early as the fourth century and has been in use in the Church in the East since the fifth century.

lifelinks

Read Acts of the Apostles 2:38, Romans 5:5, 2 Corinthians 1:21–22, and Ephesians 1:13–14. In this space describe what they tell you about the gift of the Holy Spirit.

_____

_____

_____

The Church Lives the Faith

The prophets in ancient Israel proclaimed that oppressing or even neglecting the poor and powerless violated the Covenant. The Catholic Church today through her social teaching speaks of a "preferential option for the poor" and calls every one of us to be witnesses of God's loving presence in the world. The Cristo Rey Network of schools is an excellent example of what great things can happen when Jesus' disciples are open to the prompting of the Holy Spirit and take action to help people in need.

The Cristo Rey Network

The Cristo Rey Network is a nationwide association of high schools that provide high-quality Catholic education to young people from low-income families who otherwise could not afford such an opportunity. Most of the students who attend a Cristo Rey school go on to college. The key to the unique character of Cristo Rey schools is a corporate internship program developed in 1996 by Cristo Rey Jesuit High School of Chicago.

Father John Foley and his fellow Jesuits started the Cristo Rey Network in 1996. They knew that there was no way students in the neighborhood could afford the nearly $9,000 a year tuition at Cristo Rey. Father Foley approached Chicago businesses, requesting internship positions for the students at Cristo Rey. The students in the internship program spend four extended days each week in class and one day at work. Whether they are doing clerical tasks, such as filing, or delivering lawyers' briefs, or helping an accountant crunch numbers, the student-intern's salary goes straight to the school toward their tuition.

The Cristo Rey Network in Chicago proved so successful and so promising that the Cassin Educational Initiative Foundation and the Bill and Melinda Gates Foundation set up a fund of more than $20 million to support the network. The funds seed feasibility studies of new schools, provide money for start-up operating costs, support networking among member schools, share best-practices activities, and pay various expenses for the network.

There are now more than a dozen religious congregations who staff Cristo Rey schools throughout the nation. Literally thousands of young people's lives have already been touched and changed by this initiative. For more on the Cristo Rey Network visit www.cristoreynetwork.org.

How is the Cristo Rey Network an example of Catholic Social Teaching being lived and making a difference?

Living the Faith
Makes a Difference

In Jesus Christ and through his saving life and work, humanity is reconciled with God. This reconciliation includes the living out of the Great Commandment, which Jesus reaffirmed and summarizes the Law of God. (See Matthew 22:34–40.) The love of God and of one's neighbor and self forms a single, inseparable command. As "anointed ones," followers of the "Anointed One," we fulfill Jesus' command to love one another (see John 13:34–35 and Matthew 25:31–46) and share in his mission of reconciliation.

Cultural Sensitivity

We live in a world in which communication technology has heightened our awareness of the world's cultural and ethnic diversity. For some, this heightened awareness gives rise to suspicion, hatred, and outright discrimination—all of which sometimes result in divisions and fears that challenge us to fulfill our mission to be reconcilers.

Developing the skills that enhance cultural sensitivity and support cultural communication can help us serve as reconcilers and agents of healing and build bridges of understanding. Using these skills can help us live Jesus' command to announce the Gospel of Salvation and reconciliation in Christ and fulfill our call to be witnesses for Christ in the world.

Here are some suggestions to help you approach other cultures with sensitivity:

❖ **Maintain an Open Mind and Heart.** Clear your mind and heart of any prejudgments (prejudices) that you might have based either on past conversations or on biased media portrayals of a particular culture.

❖ **Recognize Commonalities.** Approach others as equals. Respect all people as children of God who have been created in his image and likeness. Identify the values and beliefs that you might share with others.

❖ **Question and Listen.** Ask others about their culture and cultural traditions or why they do certain things. Learning and dialoguing about the significance of a particular custom or belief helps people grow in mutual understanding.

❖ **Involve Yourself.** Look for ways to increase your personal experiences of people and events from a variety of cultures that are different from your own. Discover and value the giftedness that people of each culture have to share with others.

❖ **Avoid Generalizations.** Recognize that only one conversation or meeting with a few people from a particular culture does not give the complete picture of a culture's way of life and its values.

❖ **Start at Home.** Take the time to honestly examine your own culture and cultural traditions.

Faith Decision

- In a small group discuss each of the suggestions for developing cultural sensitivity. Then identify how implementing each suggestion might help a person become a reconciler and healer of divisions.
- Spend time in prayer. Quietly talk to God about how he looks upon the differences among his children all over the earth. As the fruit of your prayer, identify a single attitude or behavior that you would like to change in yourself that would help you grow in respect and reverence for all people.

This week I will become a better reconciler and healer of divisions by

_____

_____

_____ .

my thoughts

In this chapter you explored the meaning of the anointing with Chrism, which is an essential element of the rite of Confirmation. You have learned that in Confirmation you will be sealed with the gift of the Holy Spirit. You will be strengthened and commissioned to be a witness for Christ, and to give your life in service to God and others as Christ, the Anointed One, did.

Write your thoughts about what God may be calling you to do as you are anointed with the Holy Spirit.

_____

_____

_____

_____

_____

_____

_____

_____

_____

_____

_____

_____

_____

A question to share with your sponsor and parents:

What has been your experience of the Holy Spirit working in your life to make you more able to share in the mission of Jesus in the world?

Chapter 6

Exchanging the Gift of Peace

Reflection on the Opening Ritual

What was your experience as you exchanged a sign of peace with others during the opening ritual?

People who have experienced genocidal war and other atrocities have come to discover that the most effective way to bring reconciliation and healing to their country is to tell the truth about what happened, let go of past wrongs, and move forward in the work of building peace. Each of us has experienced being wronged or harmed. We have had to acknowledge what happened and then let go of hurts in order to build peace. We have come to learn the meaning of Jesus' words, "Blessed are the peacemakers" (Matthew 5:9).

What is the importance of letting go of hurts in the process of building peace?

65

The Peace of God

scripture FOCUS

What is the peace that Jesus and his disciples bring to the world?

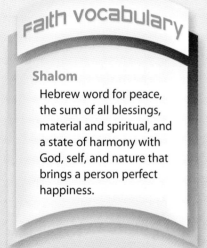

Faith vocabulary

Shalom
Hebrew word for peace, the sum of all blessings, material and spiritual, and a state of harmony with God, self, and nature that brings a person perfect happiness.

To the peoples of the ancient world that surrounded Israel, the word *peace* primarily meant "an absence of war." If you are attentive to how the word *peace* is used today in the popular media and by politicians and others, you will see that its secular meaning has not changed much in the last 3,000 years. The word *peace* in Sacred Scripture, however, has a far deeper and broader meaning.

Shalom

In the Old Testament, it is clear that the Jewish people had a very different meaning for their word for peace, **shalom,** which is used in the Old Testament nearly 280 times. Shalom had deep religious significance. It pointed to the combination of all the blessings God had bestowed and continues to bestow on his people.

Peace in the Old Testament is a gift from God that refers to a state of harmony with God and all creation. It is a happiness radiating from within a person because of the blessings of the Covenant. It is the experience of an abundance of material and spiritual blessings. There is little wonder, then, that the greeting "Peace be with you" became a regular greeting found often in the Scriptures of ancient Israel. (See 1 Samuel 25:6 and 1 Chronicles 12:19 for examples.)

Jesus, the Peace of God

The early Church came to faith in Jesus, the Prince of Peace announced by Isaiah, the One who would bring God's peace. (See Isaiah 9:5–6, 54:10, 13–14.) Jesus is the peace of God, the one who brought reconciliation to all by "making peace by the blood of his cross" (Colossians 1:20).

Luke 9:51–19:27 describes Jesus' journey to Jerusalem as a time when he teaches his followers what it means to be his disciples. At the beginning of this section of Luke's Gospel, Jesus sends seventy-two of his followers out on mission (see Luke 10:1–12), just as he had earlier sent out the Twelve (see Luke 9:1–6). He instructs them that the first thing they are to do is share shalom, the gift of God's peace, with those they greet whenever they enter a house.

> "Into whatever house you enter, first say, 'Peace to this household.' If a peaceful person lives there, your peace will rest on him; but if not, it will return to you . . . Whatever town you enter and they welcome you, eat what is set before you, cure the sick in it and say to them, 'The kingdom of God is at hand for you.'"
>
> LUKE 10:5–6, 8–9

Jesus, the Prince of Peace, associated his gift of peace with both forgiveness of sin and healing. Shalom is the sure sign that God's kingdom has come upon them. Proclaiming that reality, as representatives of Christ, is the mission and ministry of the disciples of Christ.

How is shalom like and unlike the common understanding of peace?

lifelinks

Work in a small group to look up 1 Corinthians 1:3, 2 Corinthians 1:2, Galatians 1:3, Ephesians 1:2, Philippians 1:2, Colossians 1:2, 1 Thessalonians 1:1, 1 Timothy 1:2, 2 Timothy 1:2, Titus 1:4, Philemon 3, 2 Peter 1:2, 2 John 3, Jude 1:2, and Revelation 1:4. Discuss what these greetings say about being disciples of Christ.

_____

_____

_____

The Peace of Christ

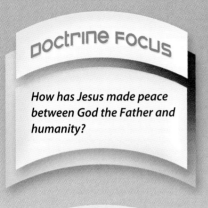

Doctrine Focus

How has Jesus made peace between God the Father and humanity?

Faith Vocabulary

encyclical
A formal letter about doctrinal or moral teaching or another aspect of the life of the Church written by the Pope or under the authority of the Pope.

The story of Adam and Eve in the Book of Genesis tells about the sinful disobedience of our first parents, or Original Sin. Original Sin resulted in the loss, not only for themselves but also for all human beings, of the original holiness and justice that our first parents had received from God.

Original Sin alienated our first parents and the human race from God. That alienation then spread and affected the relationships of people with one another and all of creation, as the stories of Cain and Abel (Genesis 4:1–25), Noah and the Great Flood (Genesis 6:5–9:28), and the Tower of Babel (Genesis 11:1–9) illustrate.

A Savior Who Reconciles

The story of the effects of this sin upon God's people and the reconciliation of God's people with him is a major theme of the Scriptures. In the Old Testament we read accounts of the way, time and time again, God sent prophets and others to his people to call them to turn away from sin and return to his love.

This work of God among his people culminated in the Father sending his only Son.

> [B]ehold, the angel of the Lord appeared to him in a dream and said, "Joseph, son of David, do not be afraid to take Mary your wife into your home. For it is through the holy Spirit that this child has been conceived in her. She will bear a son and you are to name him Jesus, because he will save his people from their sins." All this took place to fulfill what the Lord had said through the prophet.   MATTHEW 1:20–22

The name *Jesus* means "God saves." After the Resurrection—once they had been filled with the gift of the Holy Spirit—the disciples began to proclaim that Jesus was the Messiah, the long-awaited Savior.

Incarnation, stained glass.

The Gospel of Peace

The Apostles and Evangelists used the word *peace* to sum up the saving work of Jesus and preached "the gospel of peace" (Ephesians 6:15). At the beginning of Luke's Gospel, Zechariah, the father of Saint John the Baptist, prophesied that the child yet to be born of Mary would "guide our feet into the path of peace" (Luke 1:79). The last book of the New Testament, Revelation, opens with the greeting:

> [P]eace from him who is and who was
> and who is to come, and from . . .
> Jesus Christ . . . who loves us and
> has freed us from our sins by his blood.
> REVELATION 1:4–5

The peace of Christ is always bound up with the gift of the Holy Spirit, whose presence in our lives makes it real. Saint Paul says, "May the God of hope fill you with all joy and peace . . . by the power of the holy Spirit" (Romans 15:13). Reborn of water and the Holy Spirit, the baptized are to live together in peace and harmony, so that the world might come to faith in Jesus, the source of all peace.

Blessed Pope John XXIII signing his encyclical *Pacem in Terris*, April 11, 1963.

In 1963, at the height of the Cold War between the USSR and the USA, Blessed Pope John XXIII wrote the **encyclical** *Pacem in Terris* (*Peace on Earth*). Pope John XXIII reminded us of the importance of proclaiming both in word and deed the peace of Christ. He called on all citizens and nations to reestablish a society based on justice, rights, and responsibilities as the foundations of peace in the world. *Pacem in Terris* still stands as an impassioned prophetic call to reshape the world as the Prince of Peace meant it to be.

What are some examples of how the authors of the New Testament used the word peace *to describe Jesus and the work he was sent to do?*

lifelinks

Take a few moments to imagine a world filled with peace and what that would look like. Then discuss with a partner who the leaders of peace are today and what you can do to respond to your baptismal call to live as a peacemaker, a child of God.

_____

_____

_____

The Sign of Peace

Faith vocabulary

Sign of Peace
One of the Church's most ancient liturgical rituals in which Christians share with one another a gesture and a prayer that the blessings of Christ's peace come upon them.

Given the significance that the word *peace* had among the ancient Jews and the members of the early Church, it is not surprising that a special ritual for sharing peace arose within the gatherings of the early Church for worship. The ritual we know as the **Sign of Peace** can be traced back in our earliest liturgical sources. Saint Paul may have been referring to this liturgical tradition when he wrote, "Greet one another with a holy kiss" (Roman 16:16).

The Kiss of Peace

One of the earliest descriptions of the liturgy of the Church is found in the writings of Saint Justin, an early martyr of the Church in Rome. Writing around the year 150, he says, in a passage describing how Christians celebrated the Eucharist, that after the prayers in common (Prayer of the Faithful) "we greet one another with a kiss."

A little more than fifty years later a document called the *Apostolic Tradition*, which was written by Saint Hippolytus in the third century, describes a more elaborate custom led by the bishop in the liturgy of initiation. Hippolytus reports that just after a candidate has been confirmed with the oil of thanksgiving:

[the bishop] will then mark them with the sign on the forehead, then give them a kiss, saying "The Lord be with you." The person marked with the sign will answer: "And with your spirit." He is to do this for each one. When they have prayed, let them offer the kiss of peace.

Saint Justin (left), detail from stained glass.

Sometime around the year 350, Saint Cyril in a series of sermons talked about the meaning of the ceremonies that the neophytes, or those newly initiated into the Church, had experienced at their Baptism, Confirmation, and First Eucharist during the Easter Vigil. Saint Cyril described the meaning of the Sign of Peace, then referred to as the Kiss of Peace, which was received right after the anointing with oil as it is today. Cyril wrote:

> This kiss unites souls, it requires that we forget all grudges. This is why Christ said: "If you are presenting your gift at the altar, and there you remember that your brother has a grievance against you, leave your offering there before the altar, and go first to be reconciled to your brother, then return and present your offering" (Matthew 5:23–24). The kiss, then, is an act of reconciliation. That is why it is holy, as blessed Paul proclaims it to be when he says, "Greet one another with a holy kiss" (1 Corinthians 16:20).

MYSTAGOGICAL CATECHESES 23, 3

What did Cyril want the new Christians to understand about the meaning of the Sign, or Kiss, of Peace?

LITURGY LINK

The rite of Confirmation is very specific in its direction that immediately after the candidate has been anointed, the bishop is to say, "Peace be with you," and the newly confirmed person is to respond, "And also with you." The Latin text of the newly confirmed person's response is literally "And with your spirit" (27).

lifelinks

Think about your relationships with your family, friends, and others. Who might you need to be reconciled with, or make peace with, before your Confirmation? What steps might you take to make this possible?

_____

_____

_____

The Church Lives the Faith

The Catholic Church in the United States of America is putting the Gospel of peace into action in many ways. One exciting way that this is happening is through the Peacebuilders Initiative. The Peacebuilders Initiative is rooted in the Church's mission of peacemaking and reconciliation and is inspired by the vision and passion of Joseph Cardinal Bernardin, the Archbishop of Chicago, who died in 1996.

Peacebuilders Initiative

Peacebuilders Initiative seeks to foster a new generation of young Catholic leaders. Each summer, forty high school students begin a yearlong, life-changing program that offers in-depth knowledge and hands-on experience in becoming a peacebuilder. Located in a culturally diverse urban setting on the Hyde Park campus of the Catholic Theological Union in Chicago, this integrated program of study, ministry, prayer, and reflection challenges participants to think critically, ask tough theological questions, and deepen their understanding of the Catholic faith. Participants learn the skills necessary for leadership, conflict resolution, and peacemaking. They profit from the resources and experience of mentors who become important role models and companions.

Each day of the program begins with morning prayer, which is followed by participants exploring the Church's understanding of peace. In the afternoon, teams of participants and mentors are sent to ministry sites throughout Chicago to see firsthand conflict transformation and peacebuilding. Participants work side-by-side with men and women who have dedicated themselves to the Church's work of peacebuilding and reconciliation in urban settings. In the evening the participants meet in small groups for faith sharing and reflect on the day. Community building and social time are essential components of this program. Participants are given plenty of fun activities throughout the week so that true friendship and fellowship can develop.

Participation in the Peacebuilders Initiative does not end after the summer session. Over the course of the year participants create and develop projects to advance peacebuilding and reconciliation in their schools, parishes, or communities. If you would like to learn more about the Peacebuilders Initiative, you can visit their Web site at www.peacebuildersinitiative.org.

What are the key elements of the Peacebuilders Initiative? Why would participation in the Peacebuilders Initiative help you live the Gospel of peace?

Living the Faith
Makes a Difference

In the Letter to the Galatians, Saint Paul contrasts the "works of the flesh" (5:19) with "the fruit of the Spirit" (5:22, 23). This passage is the origin of the Church's tradition of listing twelve Fruits of the Holy Spirit, namely: charity, joy, peace, patience, kindness, goodness, generosity, gentleness, faithfulness, modesty, self-control, and chastity. (See *Catechism of the Catholic Church* 1832.)

Peace of Mind

Scripture scholars point out that the word *peace* as it appears in the list of the Fruits of the Holy Spirit in Galatians has a distinctively Christian meaning not found in Jewish or pagan literature. The meaning of *peace* as a Fruit of the Holy Spirit is "serenity," or "peace of mind."

Catholic tradition offers a wonderfully rich set of resources to help you achieve this inner peace of mind. One of these resources is contemplative prayer. Saint Teresa of Avila describes contemplative prayer as "taking time . . . to be alone with him who we know loves us." In contemplative prayer a person uses few words and is simply alone with God and is present to the movement of the Holy Spirit in their life. (See *Catechism of the Catholic Church* 2709–2724.)

Lectio divina is a kind of contemplative prayer. It is an ancient way of praying over the Word of God contained in the Bible. Although lectio divina began and developed in monasteries of men and women, it is a simple way of praying that just about anyone can use.

◆ Begin in silence, move away from the concerns and worries and busyness of life.

◆ Place yourself in God's presence.

◆ Select a part of the Bible, maybe a Gospel passage or a Psalm verse.

◆ Read it slowly. You may wish to read it out loud. Some people have found that writing or copying out the passage of Scripture helps them to slow down. It is important not to rush.

◆ As something strikes you—an image, a word, a teaching—stop and dwell with that. Let God's Word take hold of you.

◆ After you feel you have finished with that particular word or verse, move on but slowly. Saint Benedict said, "*Non multa, sed multum*," "Not many verses, but go into depth with what you have before you."

◆ When you are finished with this time of prayer, offer God a prayer of thanksgiving.

You can learn more about lectio divina by visiting the Web site www.ocarm.org/lectio.

Faith Decision

- Spend some time discussing:

  —Why is keeping silent difficult for many people?

  —What might it be like to be silent for an extended period of time—an hour, a day, a weekend?

- Think about when you might spend silent time during the week being simply alone with God—without your television, music, computer, or other distractions—to pray using lectio divina.

This week I will prayerfully read the Bible using lectio divina and listen to God in the silence of contemplation at the following time:

_____

_____

_____

my thoughts

In this chapter you learned about the meaning of shalom, or God's gift of peace. You explored the significance of the exchange of a sign of peace in the rite of Confirmation and how it expresses one of the effects of the outpouring of the Holy Spirit, namely, peace. Such peace is the restoration of our friendship with God. It is one of the Fruits of the Holy Spirit's presence in our lives. It overflows into a way of living that makes us peacemakers.

Write your thoughts about the gift of peace. How have you already experienced peace in your life, and how do you long for a greater experience of it as one of the effects of being confirmed?

_____

_____

_____

_____

_____

_____

_____

_____

_____

_____

_____

_____

A question to share with your sponsor and parents:

What has been your experience of peace resulting from the Holy Spirit's presence with you and working in your life?

chapter 7

Sharing in the Eucharist

Reflection on the Opening Ritual

What was your experience as you shared the bread in the opening ritual and connected with those who are suffering?

In the days immediately following the destruction of the Twin Towers of the World Trade Center in New York City on September 11, 2001, citizens throughout the world felt a deep and powerful solidarity, or connection, with the victims and their loved ones. We stood in solidarity, held candlelight vigils, shared their pain, and came to realize how deeply interconnected we are with one another.

In what way does your own experience of solidarity with those who suffer help you better understand the sacrifice of Jesus for our sins?

Catholic University of America students, candlelight vigil, Capitol Reflecting Pool, Washington D.C., September 11, 2002.

The Bread of Affliction

scripture FOCUS

How does a history of innocent suffering link the Jewish Passover and the Eucharist?

Faith vocabulary

Passover

The Jewish feast that celebrates the sparing of the Israelites from death, and God's saving his people from slavery in Egypt and leading them to freedom in the land he promised them.

Lamb of God, detail from stained glass.

Because the Last Supper takes place in the context of the Jewish **Passover** celebration, it is essential for us to know about and understand this celebration. In this way we can come to understand the meaning of the Eucharistic sacrifice. The Hebrew word for Passover, *pesah*, is translated *pascha* in Greek. The four Gospels clearly link the Paschal Mystery of Jesus' Passion, death, Resurrection, and glorious Ascension with the Passover.

The Lamb of God

Each year the Jewish people gather and celebrate the saving events of YHWH sparing the Israelites from death and saving them from slavery in Egypt and leading them safely to the land he promised them. Integral to these saving events was the slaughter of the passover, or paschal, lamb, whose blood marked the doorposts of the homes of the Israelites. This signaled the Lord to "pass over that door and not let the destroyer come into your houses" (Exodus 12:23).

Saint John the Baptist identified Jesus to be "the Lamb of God, who takes away the sin of the world" (John 1:29). The innocent blood of Jesus has once and for all delivered humanity from the slavery of sin and power of death. Jesus willingly offered himself up in our place as a sacrifice on the cross.

On Passover the Jews eat unleavened bread and bitter herbs, the bread of affliction, to remind them of the painful past of their deliverance. This imagery of the "bread of affliction" paints the background of our Eucharistic joy as well. Just as the Passover remains a joyful feast for the Jews, the Eucharist is a joy for Christians. Jesus' Resurrection and Ascension is a foreshadowing of our own deliverance in the Promised Land of heaven. In the Eucharist, we share in the Body and Blood of Christ, the Lamb of God who takes away the sins of both the living and dead. We enter more deeply into communion with God and receive the pledge of the glory to come.

An Offering of Love

In the narrative of the Last Supper in John's Gospel, there is no mention of Jesus offering the bread and wine as his Body and Blood. Instead, John's Gospel describes Jesus washing the disciples' feet. Many Scripture scholars see this as John's way of describing the meaning of Jesus instituting the Eucharist.

Jesus Dismisses Judas, from *Life of Jesus* series. William Hole, nineteenth-century British artist.

John's Gospel includes a significant detail in this account. In Jesus' time there was a custom of the dinner host dipping a piece of bread and offering it to one of the guests as a special sign of honor or affection. Jesus used this custom to make a last appeal to Judas Iscariot to change his mind about betraying him. After describing Jesus washing the disciples' feet, John's Gospel continues:

> Jesus was deeply troubled and testified, "Amen, amen, I say to you, one of you will betray me." The disciples looked at one another, at a loss as to whom he meant. One of his disciples, the one whom Jesus loved, was reclining at Jesus' side. So Simon Peter nodded to him to find out whom he meant. He leaned back against Jesus' chest and said to him, "Master, who is it?" Jesus answered, "It is the one to whom I hand the morsel after I have dipped it." So he dipped the morsel and [took it and] handed it to Judas, son of Simon the Iscariot. After he took the morsel, Satan entered him. So Jesus said to him, "What you are going to do, do quickly." So he took the morsel and left at once. And it was night.
>
> JOHN 13:21–27, 30

What common themes are present in both the Jewish Passover and the Eucharist?

lifelinks

Imagine that you are one of the disciples, other than Judas Iscariot, at the Last Supper. Describe your thoughts and feelings as Jesus speaks to Judas.

_____

_____

_____

Participation in the Eucharist

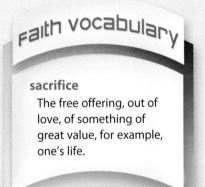

Faith Vocabulary

sacrifice
The free offering, out of love, of something of great value, for example, one's life.

The Bible is filled with accounts of people's life-changing encounters with God. Often those meetings took place during a meal or were followed by or commemorated in a meal. Such stories are the background for the meal in Emmaus during which two disciples recognized the Risen Lord in the breaking of the bread. (See Luke 24:29–31.) The Eucharist is meant to be that kind of meal for us, too—one in which we meet Christ who transforms us and changes our lives.

Eucharist: Life-Changing Encounter

Luke's Gospel tells us that the two disciples listened attentively to Christ and asked for him to stay with them for the evening. They were involved in their encounter with the Risen Christ. Our participation in the Eucharist requires that same attention to Christ, who is present with us.

There are two sides to every life-changing encounter with the Mystery of God: God's part and our response. God is present and active at every Eucharist celebration in many ways—in the Scripture, the assembly, the priest, and, in a unique way, in the Body and Blood of Christ.

The Eucharistic Prayer speaks of God's presence as the work of the Holy Spirit, who is invoked, not only over both bread and wine, but over us as well. The priest prays to the Father:

> Look with favor on your
>   Church's offering,
> and see the victim whose
>   death has reconciled
>   us to yourself.
> Grant that we, who are
>   nourished by his body
>   and blood,
> may be filled with his
>   Holy Spirit,
> and become one body,
>   one spirit in Christ.
> Eucharistic Prayer III

One Mind and Heart with Christ

The power of the Holy Spirit is at work in the Eucharist to deepen our union with Christ, separate us from sin, deepen our unity with the Mystical Body of Christ, the Church, and commit us to the poor. What is required of us in order for this life-changing encounter to take place? Like the two disciples from Emmaus, we must enter deeply into the mystery made present at every Eucharist. We must join ourselves to Christ, and out of love and obedience, offer ourselves as a living **sacrifice** to the Father. We must have the same attitude of mind and heart as Jesus: an attitude of self-offering and commitment to stand in solidarity with all those for whom Jesus died.

Full, conscious, and active participation in the Eucharist refers not just to our external behaviors at Mass—listening, responding to prayers, singing, and so on. It requires us to have certain internal dispositions, or habits, of mind and heart by which God guides us to be aware of what is happening inside of us and to be of one mind and heart with Christ. Both our external and internal dispositions help us join with Christ in freely giving ourselves over to God the Father with the same spirit of love and obedience as he did.

What is the role of the Holy Spirit at Eucharist? What is our role?

Liturgy Link

Each of the sacraments has special graces, or transforming effects, for our life. One of the special graces of the Eucharist connects us to the poor and suffering and demands that we stand in solidarity with them and act on their behalf. "The Eucharist commits us to the poor. To receive in truth the Body and Blood of Christ given up for us, we must recognize Christ in the poorest, his brethren" (*Catechism of the Catholic Church* 1397).

lifelinks

In a small group make a list of the internal and external dispositions that are required for a person's full, conscious, and active participation in the Eucharist. In your journal write what you can do to develop these dispositions.

_____

_____

_____

The Church
Lives the Faith

One of the fruits, or special graces, of our participation in the Eucharist is the grace "to recognize Christ in the poorest" of our brothers and sisters. The bishops of the United States help us respond to that grace in many ways. One way is through our participation in the work of Catholic Relief Services (CRS). These efforts give substance to the Church's insistence that "the Eucharist commits us to the poor" (*Catechism of the Catholic Church* 1397).

CRS distribution of seeds to grow crops, Kaunga Mashi village, Zambia, near border of Angola.

Catholic Relief Services

An excellent example of the way that Catholic Relief Services stands in solidarity with the poor of the world is their work in Niger, one of the poorest nations in the entire world. Niger, in West Africa's Sahara region, is four-fifths the size of Alaska. Sixty-three percent of the country's 12.5 million people live on less than one U.S. dollar a day. According to UNICEF, United Nations Children's Fund, 40 percent of Niger's children are malnourished, and 84 percent of the adult population cannot read or write.

CRS distribution of food during a famine and drought, Mungus, Zambia.

Catholic Relief Services has been working in Niger since 1991. Guided by the values expressed in the social teachings of the Catholic Church, Catholic Relief Services' work in Niger includes these and other programs:

- ❖ Food for Work: CRS sponsors Food for Work activities that help over 40,000 households learn sustainable agriculture techniques, improve local infrastructure, and feed their families during times of hunger.
- ❖ Food Security: CRS works with other international organizations and local partners to promote sustainable agriculture, natural resource management, and improved health and nutrition in 120 villages.
- ❖ Nomad Education: CRS, in partnership with the Catholic Church and World Food Program, runs an education project helping nomad children access quality primary education.

Nutrition education at CRS mother/child health clinic, Hangar village, near Bembereke, Benin.

An example of how these programs work is illustrated by CRS's working with the poor of Niger in 2004 to respond to a severe locust outbreak and subsequent drought. The double blow destroyed nearly 80 percent of crops, resulting in some families eating leaves, grasses, and the seeds they would have planted during the growing season. CRS and its partners distributed food rations to over 40,000 families and provided therapeutic feeding to 7,000 malnourished children. CRS and its partners also distributed vouchers that would enable households to access animal feed, seeds, and planting tools in preparation for the planting season. Read more about Catholic Relief Services at www.crs.org.

How is the work of CRS an example of the Catholic Church taking seriously the connection between the Eucharist and the solidarity of the Church with the poor?

CRS/World Food Program distribution of food, Tolkobeye, Niger.

Living the Faith
Makes a Difference

S.O.M.E. (So Others Might Eat) youth and adult leaders, Washington, D.C. soup kitchen for homeless people.

At Confirmation you will be sealed with the gift of the Holy Spirit. Confirmation imprints a spiritual mark, or indelible character, on your soul. For this reason Confirmation may be received only one time. You will be led to a deeper initiation into the Body of Christ, the Church, and a fuller participation in the Eucharist. This empowers you to take part more closely in the mission of the Church and to "bear witness to the Christian faith in words accompanied by deed" (*Catechism of the Catholic Church* 1317).

Bearing Witness to the Christian Faith

Our solidarity with the poor, which is one of the fruits of Holy Communion, is another name for "bearing witness to the Christian faith." The Sermon on the Mount in chapter 5 of Matthew's Gospel presents a vision and summary of how the disciples of Jesus are to bear witness to their faith in him. These actions are key to what it means for you to participate in the Eucharist at a deep level—not simply by attending Mass, but by fully, actively, and consciously participating in the Eucharistic celebration and by fully, actively, and consciously living out its meaning in your life every day.

Eagle scout and friends painting a community building, Jacksonville, Florida.

FaITH DECISION

Work in a small group to fill out the chart.

- Look up and read the Beatitudes in Matthew 5:3–11. Discuss the meaning of each of the Beatitudes.
- Choose three of the Beatitudes. Write one of the Beatitudes you have chosen in each of the spaces in the left column.
- In the spaces in the center column restate each in contemporary language so that your peers can more clearly understand the meaning of Jesus' words.
- In the spaces in the right column write concrete and realistic ways you can live each of the Beatitudes.

The Beatitude	Beatitude in Contemporary Language	Beatitude in Action

This week I will live the Beatitudes more fully by

_____

_____

_____ .

my thoughts

In this chapter you learned why the rite of Confirmation is most appropriately celebrated within Mass. You explored how the gift of the Holy Spirit empowers you to participate in the Eucharist more fully, consciously, and actively. You discovered the implications that participation in the Eucharist has for your solidarity with the poor and powerless of this world.

Reflect on and write any new understandings you have of the Eucharist and how participation in the Eucharist is connected to your Confirmation.

_____

_____

_____

_____

_____

_____

_____

_____

_____

_____

_____

A question to share with your sponsor and parents:

What has been your experience of the connection between sharing in the Eucharist and standing in solidarity with poor and powerless people?

Sending Forth on Mission

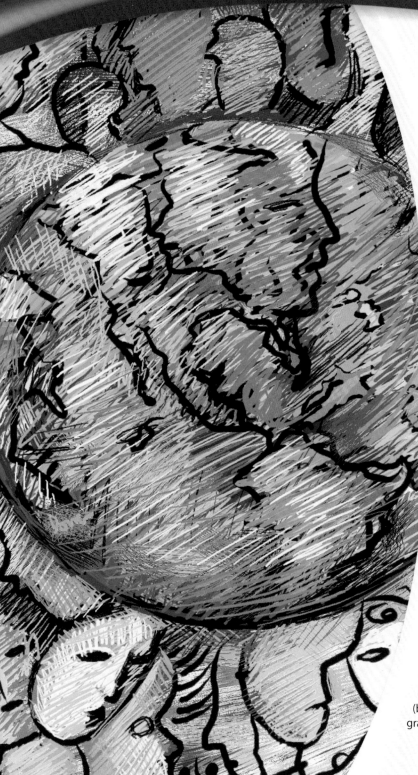

Reflection on the Opening Ritual

What was your experience as you listened to the public witness during the opening ritual?

The media are filled with people who offer public witness to various experiences. Celebrities, athletes, politicians, and business people embrace causes and share how their lives have been changed by their new commitments. Every day actors, doctors, and other people endorse some new product by praising its amazing effects.

From your experience, what is the most effective way that a person can publicly witness to their faith in Jesus?

Green World #2. Diana Ong (b. 1940), Chinese-American graphic artist.

Transformed by the Holy Spirit

Faith Vocabulary

Sanhedrin
The supreme governing council of the Jewish people during Jesus' time.

Resurrection
The bodily raising of Jesus from the dead on the third day of his death on the cross and burial in a tomb to a new and glorified life, an event historically attested to by the disciples who really encountered the Risen One.

The Church is the Temple of the Holy Spirit. Saint Luke deliberately shows in the Acts of the Apostles how the Holy Spirit who animated Jesus' ministry continues to be present in the Church. Luke does this by using a mirroring technique. By this technique Luke describes in the Acts of the Apostles events that are similar to what he has previously narrated in his Gospel. This is Luke's way of saying to his readers that the Holy Spirit lives on in the Church, continuing the ministry that Jesus entrusted to his disciples.

Bold Witness for Christ

Jesus is truly alive in his Church. Saint Luke attests both to the fact that the disciples of Jesus encountered the Risen Lord and to the amazing effect those encounters had on the disciples after they received the gift of the Holy Spirit on Pentecost. The very disciples who ran away from Jesus in fear during his final hours are suddenly filled with courage. They become fearless and bold witnesses to the fact that Jesus has been raised from the dead. Scholars point out that Luke's use of the Greek word for bold is his shorthand way of emphasizing the presence of the Holy Spirit at work in the disciples.

After presenting Saint Peter's courageous proclamation to the Jewish pilgrims gathered in Jerusalem for the celebration of Pentecost, Luke includes in his Acts of the Apostles accounts of the Apostles performing miraculous cures and casting out demons, just as Jesus went about "doing good and healing those oppressed by the devil, for God was with him" (Acts of the Apostles 10:38). Likewise, the Apostles proclaim the arrival of God's kingdom, calling for repentance and faith in Jesus as God's Anointed One.

Saint Peter preaching, detail from stained glass.

Filled with the Holy Spirit

Chapter 4 of the Acts of the Apostles describes how the gift of the Holy Spirit transformed the frightened Apostles into bold witnesses to Jesus' Resurrection. After curing a crippled man, Saint Peter and Saint John were arrested and brought before the Jewish leaders in the Sanhedrin. The **Sanhedrin** was the supreme governing council of the Jewish people during Jesus' time. Then Saint Luke's narrative describes what happened:

> Peter, filled with the holy Spirit, answered them . . . Observing the boldness of Peter and John and perceiving them to be uneducated, ordinary men, [the Jewish leaders] were amazed, and they recognized them as the companions of Jesus. ACTS OF THE APOSTLES 4:8, 13

Saint Peter Following Saint John as He Heals the Sick with His Shadow, detail from fresco. Masaccio (1401–1428), Italian painter, Florentine School.

The Jewish leaders then discussed among themselves what to do with the Apostles and ultimately decided to release Peter and John. The two Apostles returned to "their own people" and reported what had happened. The people rejoiced and joined in prayer, saying:

> "And now, Lord, take note of their threats, and enable your servants to speak your word with all boldness, as you stretch forth (your) hand to heal, and signs and wonders are done through the name of your holy servant Jesus." As they prayed, the place where they were gathered shook, and they were all filled with the holy Spirit and continued to speak the word of God with boldness.
> ACTS OF THE APOSTLES 4:29–31

What does Saint Luke emphasize by making such a point of the boldness with which the Apostles spoke about Jesus?

lifelinks

In a small group read Acts of the Apostles 4:5–22, the entire account of Saint Peter and Saint John before the Sanhedrin. Then create a group prayer to the Holy Spirit, asking for the same boldness to proclaim the Good News.

_____

_____

_____

Our Mission as Evangelizers

Giving public witness to Jesus Christ and the Gospel is the heart of the work of all the baptized. All Salvation comes from God and has been accomplished once and for all through Jesus Christ and the Holy Spirit, and is made present in the sacred actions of the Church's liturgy, especially in the seven sacraments. The heart of our vocation as Christians lies in our mission to announce the gift of Salvation and to bring the Gospel of Jesus to the entire world. We call this work of the Church **evangelization.** Evangelization is the Church's work of sharing the Gospel with all people "so that it may enter the hearts of all [people] and renew the face of the earth."

Pope Paul VI, Eucharistic Congress, Bombay, India, December 3, 1964.

A "New Evangelization"

Pope Paul VI, who was pope from 1963 to1978, reminded the Church of the importance of this work. He wrote:

> Evangelizing is in fact the grace and vocation proper to the Church, her deepest identity. She exists in order to evangelize.　ON EVANGELIZATION IN THE MODERN WORLD 14

Evangelization is not a task reserved for a select few within the Church, such as missionaries who leave their homeland and travel to other countries. Evangelization is the task that Jesus has given to each and every one of the baptized. The responsibility of all Christians to participate in the work of evangelization flows from their initiation into the Body of Christ, the Church. The graces of Confirmation and the Eucharist deepen this responsibility and strengthen the baptized to spread the Good News.

Pope John Paul II with Jean-Claude Duvalier, President of Haiti and his wife Michelle, at airport, Port-au-Prince, Haiti, March 9, 1983.

On his first visit to Poland as Pope on June 9, 1979, Pope John Paul II first proclaimed that "A new evangelization has begun!" However, it was five years later on October 12, 1984, on the occasion of his visit to Port-au-Prince, Haiti, that he called in a more formal way for this "new evangelization." Over the next twenty-one years he explained what he meant by this "new evangelization." He described it as a commitment to spread the Gospel that would be new in the fervor with which it is pursued, the methods it employs, and the way it is expressed in various cultures.

Go and Make Disciples

In 1992 the United States Catholic bishops wrote an important national plan and strategy for evangelization. This plan, *Go and Make Disciples*, helps Catholics get a better sense of the meaning of evangelization and how they can make it real in their own lives. The three goals of Catholic evangelization named and discussed in *Go and Make Disciples* are:

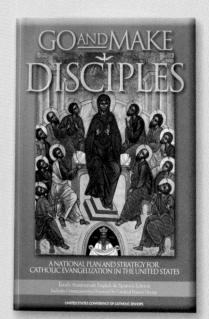

- "To bring about in all Catholics such an enthusiasm for their faith that, in living their faith in Jesus, they freely share it with others" (46).
- "To invite all people in the United States, whatever their social or cultural background, to hear the message of salvation in Jesus Christ so they may come to join us in the fullness of the Catholic faith" (53). Our bishops encourage us to invite, not to force our ideas on, others who are unwilling to hear them.
- "To foster gospel values in our society, promoting the dignity of the human person, the importance of the family, and the common good of our society, so that our nation may continue to be transformed by the saving power of Jesus Christ" (56). We must work to change our society to become more as Jesus would have it be.

All three goals are both a clear and challenging summary of Pope Paul VI's message and reflect what Pope John Paul II called the "new evangelization."

How would you summarize the three goals of evangelization spelled out in Go and Make Disciples *in your own words?*

lifelinks

Work in a small group to search the Gospels to find three passages that describe Jesus or his disciples living each of the three goals of evangelization. Decide on one practical way you can live each of the goals.

_____

_____

_____

The Church
Lives the Faith

Catholics work together to respond to the invitation and grace of the Holy Spirit to fulfill the tasks of evangelization set forth in *Go and Make Disciples*. The Paulist National Catholic Evangelization Association (PNCEA) was established in 1977 as an apostolate of the Paulist Fathers, the first order of Catholic priests established in the United States.

Paulist National Catholic Evangelization Association (PNCEA)

Paulist National Catholic Evangelization Association inspires and helps Catholics to bring the light of Christ to their families, workplaces, and neighborhoods. The members of PNCEA provide user-friendly resources to Catholic dioceses, parishes, and individuals, helping them bring the good news of Jesus Christ to a variety of people in different settings. The broad range of programs and services that PNCEA provides offers some idea of how many different ways we can fulfill the command of Jesus to share the good news of God's love.

These are eight of the resources PNCEA offers as described on their Web site, www.pncea.org:

▶ **Disciples in Mission.** "Disciples in Mission" is a three-year, parish-wide experience of evangelization.

▶ **ENVISION—Planning Our Parish Future.**
"ENVISION" is a Christ-centered pastoral
planning process that engages all
parishioners in developing and
implementing a faith-based
vision for their parish.

▶ **I am E3—Evangelizing
Every day Everywhere.**
"I am E3" is a parish resource
that stimulates one-on-one
faith sharing through the use of
conversation-starting faith stories
on attractive, easy-to-use cards.

▶ **Invite.** "Invite" is a resource that equips
members of Catholic parishes to reach out and
invite people who have no Church family to consider
joining the Catholic faith.

▶ **Catholics Reaching Out.** "Catholics Reaching Out" is
a resource that equips members of Catholic parishes
to reach out and invite inactive Catholics to return to
the active practice of the faith.

▶ **The Reconciling Community.** "The Reconciling
Community" helps Catholics invite inactive Catholics
to consider returning to the Sacrament of Penance.

▶ **Parish Missions.** "Parish Missions" brings a mission
team of a priest and a religious or laywoman to
parishes for a weeklong experience in evangelizing
spirituality.

▶ **Prison Ministries.** "Prison Ministries" helps prison
chaplains and volunteers provide inmates with solid
Catholic teaching through the use of newsletters,
Bibles, adult faith education books, and prayer cards.

If you would like to find out more about some of the
practical ways that you can live out your mission as an
evangelizer, there are other resources available on the
PNCEA Web site at www.pncea.org.

*What are some of the ways that PNCEA offers Catholics
the opportunity to be part of the Church's mission of
evangelization?*

Living the Faith
Makes a Difference

In very simple and effective ways, each of us who is a baptized and Spirit-filled follower of Jesus can develop our skills at being everyday evangelizers. *Go and Make Disciples* provides us with an exciting vision of how every member of the Catholic Church can proclaim the Gospel, invite others to become disciples of Christ, and also invite members of the Church to deepen their faith in Christ. Using the framework of the three goals set forth in *Go and Make Disciples*, think about how you can answer the call of Jesus to help spread the Gospel as he commanded, "Go, therefore, and make disciples of all nations" (Matthew 28:19).

Let Your Light Shine

Goal 1: To live and share our faith enthusiastically with others by word and witness. We have all known people whose enthusiasm is infectious. We cannot help but feel energized and interested in what they are about since they are so positive and happy. That is the kind of witness that the disciples of Jesus are meant to give to those they meet along life's journey.

Reflect on the Holy Spirit who dwells within you. Ask the Holy Spirit to fire your heart and mind with the gift and power of enthusiasm. Name a quality of a person of enthusiasm. Then decide on how you can grow in making that quality part of who you are.

Quality: _____

What I can do: _____

Goal 2: To invite others to know Jesus Christ. Many people simply need a personal invitation and may even have been silently wishing to learn more about Jesus and the Catholic Church. Inviting others to come to know Jesus Christ more deeply is about connecting them to the Church, the Body of Christ, in which Jesus continues to be present in word, in sacrament, and in a people who bear his name.

Reflect on the presence of Jesus with you. Ask the Lord Jesus to help you grow as a person of Christian hospitality, a person who extends an invitation to others to come to know Christ better. Name a quality of a person of Christian hospitality. Then decide on how you can grow in making that quality part of who you are.

Quality: _____

What I can do: _____

Goal 3: To help transform the world in Christ. The social teachings of the Catholic Church guide us in the work of the transformation of the world in Christ. Review the "Basic Principles of Catholic Social Teaching" on page 116. Reflect on how you are living one of these principles. Then decide on how you make the principles of Catholic Social Teaching part of your everyday life to help transform the world in Christ.

Principle: _____

_____

What I can do: _____

_____

FAITH DECISION

- Work in a small group to identify several concrete ways a person your age can work with others to transform the world in Christ.

- Choose one of those ways and work with others to implement it.

This week I will take part in the Church's work of evangelization by

_____

_____

_____

_____ .

my thoughts

In this chapter you learned about the last part of the celebration of Confirmation, the sending forth at the conclusion of the Eucharistic liturgy. You have explored the rich symbolism and meaning of the dismissal command, *Ite missa est*, by which the assembly is sent forth to share the good news of God's love. In the rite of Confirmation you will be sealed with the gift of the Holy Spirit in order to take part in the Church's mission of evangelization. Those words of dismissal, therefore, are meant for you in a very direct way.

Reflect on the words of the dismissal command and write your thoughts about the ways that you are sent forth from Mass each week to evangelize.

A question to share with your sponsor and parents:

What has been your experience of sharing God's Good News with others?

Chapter 1

We Gather in Jesus' Name

Ritual Action: Gathering in Procession

All: *Walk in procession and gather in a circle around the prayer center.*

Leader: Jesus promised that whenever we gather in his name, he is in our midst. With this in mind, we begin with the Sign of the Cross.

All: *All sign themselves.*

Leader: Let us bow our heads as we remember that the Lord is with us in this moment of prayer. *(Pause.)*

Lord Jesus, you have called us as your own in Baptism, and you have gathered us here this day to understand more deeply the mystery of your love for us. Show us how to gather in your name, so that we might worship you in spirit and in truth. You who live and reign, for ever and ever.

All: **Amen.**

Scripture Reading

Reader: A reading from the holy gospel according to Luke.

All: **Glory to you, O Lord.**

Reader: *Proclaim Luke 4:16–22a. Conclude by saying,* The gospel of the Lord.

All: **Praise to you, Lord Jesus Christ.**

Prayer of Intercession

Leader: Let us offer our prayers now, filled with faith in God's goodness.

Reader: For all who will have no food or shelter this night, let us pray to the Lord:

All: **Lord, hear our prayer.**

Reader: For those who are in prison and without hope for the future, let us pray to the Lord:

All: **Lord, hear our prayer.**

Reader: For those who are dying, and for those who gather in prayer at their bedsides, let us pray to the Lord:

All: **Lord, hear our prayer.**

Reader: For candidates throughout the world who are preparing for the Sacrament of Confirmation, and for their sponsors and their families, let us pray to the Lord:

All: **Lord, hear our prayer.**

Reader: Let us now pray in silence for our personal intentions. *(Pause.)* Let us pray to the Lord:

All: **Lord, hear our prayer.**

Closing

Leader: Let us pray together the prayer that Jesus taught.

All: **Our Father . . .**

Chapter 2

Listening to the Word of God

Gathering

All: *Gather in the prayer area.*

Leader: Jesus promised that whenever we gather in his name he is in our midst. With this in mind, we begin with the Sign of the Cross.

All: *All sign themselves.*

Leader: Let us bow our heads as we remember that the Lord is with us in this moment of prayer. *(Pause.)*

All-powerful God, in the fullness of time, you spoke your Word who took on human flesh and saved us from our sins. Speak to us now in a living word, a word that touches our hearts and fills us with love. We ask this in the name of Jesus your Son, the Living Word come down from heaven, who lives and reigns for ever and ever.

All: **Amen.**

Scripture Reading

Leader: Let us listen now to the inspired words of Scripture with faith-filled hearts, remembering that through these words it is God himself who speaks to us. Let our hearts be fertile soil, receptive to the seeds that are planted today by these words of Salvation.
Pause briefly before handing the Bible to the first reader.

Reader 1: A reading from the Book of Deuteronomy.
Proclaim Deuteronomy 28:1, 2.
Pause briefly before handing the Bible to the next reader.

Reader 2: A reading from the Book of Isaiah.
Proclaim Isaiah 55:10, 11.
Pause briefly before handing the Bible to the next reader.

Reader 3: A reading from the Gospel of Matthew.
Proclaim Matthew 13:3–9.
Pause briefly before handing the Bible to the next reader.

Reader 4: A reading from the Gospel of John.
Proclaim John 6:63, 68.

Communal Response

Leader: Let us respond to God's word by saying together: Your words, O God, are Spirit and light.

All: **Your words, O God, are Spirit and light.**

Leader: Your word, LORD, stands forever; / it is firm as the heavens. / Through all generations your truth endures.
PSALM 119:89, 90

All: **Your words, O God, are Spirit and light.**

Leader: Your word is a lamp for my feet, / a light for my path. / I make a solemn vow / to keep your just edicts.   PSALM 119:105–106

All: **Your words, O God, are Spirit and light.**

Leader: I call to you to save me / that I may keep your decrees. / I rise before dawn and cry out; / I put my hope in your words.
PSALM 119:146, 147

All: **Your words, O God, are Spirit and light.**

Ritual Action: Reverencing God's Word

Leader: Let us now express by some visible sign how much the Word of God means to us. Please approach the enthroned Bible and with a special awareness and prayerfulness, reverence it by kissing it, tracing a cross on it, or offering some other expression of your reverence for God's word.

All: *Come forward and reverence the Word of God.*

Closing

Leader: Let us pray together the prayer that Jesus taught.

All: **Our Father . . .**

Chapter 3

Recalling Our Baptism

Gathering

All: *Gather in the prayer area.*

Leader: Jesus promised that whenever we gather in his name, he is in our midst. With this in mind, we begin with the Sign of the Cross, invoking the Holy Trinity, in whose name we were baptized.

All: *All sign themselves.*

Leader: Let us bow our heads as we remember that the Lord is with us in this moment of prayer. *(Pause.)*

Lord Jesus, at your baptism in the Jordan River, the Father sent the Holy Spirit upon you in the form of a dove, as a sign that you are his beloved Son. Help us today to be mindful of our Baptism, when we were chosen as beloved children of the Father, anointed with the Holy Spirit, and given a share in your risen life. We ask you this, Lord Jesus, who lives and reigns for ever and ever.

All: **Amen.**

Scripture Reading

Leader: Jesus has told us that he came to give us the gift of eternal life. That life is first offered to us in the Sacrament of Baptism. Listen now to the final words of Jesus to his disciples before he ascended into heaven.

Reader: A reading from the holy gospel according to Matthew.

All: **Glory to you, O Lord.**

Reader: *Proclaim Matthew 28:18–20. Conclude by saying,* The gospel of the Lord.

All: **Praise to you, Lord Jesus Christ.**

Prayer of Intercession

Leader: We pray for those who are not allowed to practice their faith openly, as well as all people who struggle to be faithful to their baptismal vows.

Reader: For all members of the Church who risk persecution or death by practicing their faith, let us pray to the Lord:

All: **Lord, hear our prayer.**

Reader: For all members of the Church who are in prison for publicly professing their faith, let us pray to the Lord:

All: **Lord, hear our prayer.**

Reader: For catechumens preparing for Baptism, especially here in our own parish, let us pray to the Lord:

All: **Lord, hear our prayer.**

Reader: For candidates throughout the world who are preparing for the Sacrament of Confirmation, and for their sponsors and their families, let us pray to the Lord:

All: **Lord, hear our prayer.**

Reader: For parents bringing their infants to be baptized, as they prepare to renew their own baptismal promises, let us pray to the Lord:

All: **Lord, hear our prayer.**

Reader: Let us now pray in silence for our personal intentions. *(Pause.)* Let us pray to the Lord:

All: **Lord, hear our prayer.**

Ritual Action: Blessing with Holy Water

Leader: Let us express our desire to renew the grace of our Baptism by signing ourselves with holy water. Please approach the holy water and with a special awareness and prayerfulness bless yourself.

All: ***Come forward and bless yourself using the holy water.***

Closing

Leader: Let us pray together the prayer that Jesus taught.

All: **Our Father . . .**

Chapter 4

Receiving a Blessing

Gathering

All: *Gather in the prayer area.*

Leader: Jesus promised that whenever we gather in his name, he is in our midst. With this in mind, we begin with the Sign of the Cross.

All: *All sign themselves.*

Leader: Let us bow our heads and remember that the Lord is with us in this moment of prayer. *(Pause.)*

Gentle Jesus, the Gospels tell us how you gathered the children to yourself, laying your hands on them and blessing them. You also laid hands on the sick and others possessed by demons, dispelling all evils of body and spirit. Lay your hands on us this day, loving Lord, and renew within us the gift of your Holy Spirit, poured out in our hearts on the day of our Baptism. We ask you this, who lives and reigns for ever and ever.

All: **Amen.**

Scripture Reading

Leader: The Book of Genesis describes how Jacob on his deathbed confers a special blessing on Ephraim and Manasseh by laying his hands on their heads. Let us now listen to these inspired words of Scripture with faith-filled hearts, remembering that through these words God himself speaks to us today.

Reader: A reading from the Book of Genesis. *Proclaim Genesis 48:13–16. Conclude by saying,* The word of the Lord.

All: **Thanks be to God.**

Ritual Action: Laying On of Hands

Leader: The ancient tradition of our ancestors in faith has been to confer a blessing while laying hands on someone's head. I invite each of you to come forward to receive a blessing. I will place my hands on your head as a sign of blessing and that we are holding you in prayer in a special way as you prepare to receive the gift of the Holy Spirit in the Sacrament of Confirmation. We will pray silently together asking for God's blessing and conclude by saying, "Amen." *Place hands on heads of each candidate.*

All: **Come forward to receive a blessing. Amen.**

Closing

Leader: Let us pray together the prayer that Jesus taught.

All: **Our Father . . .**

Chapter 5

The Gift of the Holy Spirit

Gathering

All: *Gather in the prayer area.*

Leader: Jesus promised that whenever we gather in his name, he is in our midst. With this in mind, we begin with the Sign of the Cross.

All: *All sign themselves.*

Leader: Let us bow our heads and remember that the Lord is with us in this moment of prayer. *(Pause.)*

Come, Holy Spirit, fill the hearts of your faithful, and kindle in them the fire of your love. Send forth your Spirit and they shall be created, and you will renew the face of the earth. We ask this through Jesus Christ our Lord, who lives and reigns for ever and ever.

All: **Amen.**

Scripture Reading

Leader: The account of Pentecost tells us not only what happened to the first disciples of Jesus. It also teaches us that the Holy Spirit is at work in our lives. Let us listen to how the gift of the Holy Spirit has been poured out on us and on all who are followers of Jesus Christ.

Reader: A reading from Acts of the Apostles. *Proclaim Acts of the Apostles 2:1–4. Conclude by saying,* The word of the Lord.

All: **Thanks be to God.**

Prayer of Intercession

Leader: Let us pray now for those who have been chosen by God and given a special call to serve the poor and the powerless.

Reader: For our sisters and brothers who work in developing countries and seek to improve the lives of those who live in poverty and despair, let us pray to the Lord:

All: **Lord, hear our prayer.**

Reader: For those who defend human rights, let us pray to the Lord:

All: **Lord, hear our prayer.**

Reader: For health-care workers who minister to people unable to afford medical care, let us pray to the Lord:

All: **Lord, hear our prayer.**

Reader: For those who give comfort to prisoners and their families, let us pray to the Lord:

All: **Lord, hear our prayer.**

Reader: For candidates throughout the world who are preparing for the Sacrament of Confirmation and for their sponsors and their families, let us pray to the Lord:

All: **Lord, hear our prayer.**

Reader: Let us now pray in silence for our personal intentions. *(Pause.)* Let us pray to the Lord:

All: **Lord, hear our prayer.**

Ritual Action: Blessing with Oil

Leader: At your Baptism you were anointed with sacred Chrism as a sign of the gift of the Holy Spirit that you received. Chrism will once again be used by the bishop at your Confirmation. Today we will use ordinary oil and trace the cross on your forehead, recalling your Baptism and looking forward to your Confirmation.

All: *Come forward to receive the oil on your forehead.*

Leader: *Trace a cross on the candidate's forehead with oil, saying,* May the gift of the Holy Spirit you first received at Baptism and who will strengthen you with his sevenfold Gifts at the time of your Confirmation guide and strengthen you as you prepare for Confirmation.

Closing

Leader: Let us pray together the prayer that Jesus taught.

All: **Our Father . . .**

Chapter 6

Bringing Peace to the World

Gathering

All: *Gather in the prayer area.*

Leader: Jesus promised that whenever we gather in his name he is in our midst. With this in mind, we pray the Sign of the Cross.

All: *All sign themselves.*

Leader: Let us bow our heads and remember that the Lord is with us in this moment of prayer. *(Pause.)*

Lord, make me an instrument of your peace. Where there is hatred, let me sow love; where there is injury, pardon; where there is doubt, faith; where there is despair, hope; where there is darkness, light; and where there is sadness, joy. Grant that we may not so much seek to be consoled as to console; to be understood, as to understand; to be loved as to love; for it is in giving that we receive, it is in pardoning that we are pardoned, and it is in dying that we are born to eternal life.

All: **Amen.**

Scripture Reading

Leader: In John's Gospel the gift of the Holy Spirit is given to the disciples on Easter Sunday evening. Let us listen now as John describes how that gift of the Holy Spirit brought peace to the disciples.

Reader: A reading from the holy gospel according to John.

All: **Glory to you, O Lord.**

Reader: *Proclaim John 20:19–23. Conclude by saying,* The gospel of the Lord.

All: **Praise to you, Lord Jesus Christ.**

Prayer of Intercession

Leader: As disciples of Jesus who have received the gift of the Holy Spirit in Baptism, we have been given the gift of God's peace and are commanded to bring that gift of peace to the world. Let us pray now that the world might know God's peace in more abundant measure.

Reader: For peace in the hearts of all who are troubled, lonely, or consumed by anger and a spirit of revenge, let us pray to the Lord:

All: **Lord, hear our prayer.**

Reader: For nations at war and for those who think that recourse to violence is the way to peace, let us pray to the Lord:

All: **Lord, hear our prayer.**

Reader: For families scarred by domestic strife, let us pray to the Lord:

All: **Lord, hear our prayer.**

Reader: For young people caught up in gangs and other movements that use violence as a way to solve problems, let us pray to the Lord:

All: **Lord, hear our prayer.**

Reader: For candidates throughout the world who are preparing for the Sacrament of Confirmation and for their sponsors and their families, let us pray to the Lord:

All: **Lord, hear our prayer.**

Reader: Let us now pray in silence for our personal intentions. *(Pause.)* Let us pray to the Lord:

All: **Lord, hear our prayer.**

Ritual Action: A Sign of Peace

Leader: Jesus told his disciples that before bringing their gift to the altar, they should go first and be reconciled with anyone with whom they are not at peace. Every time we participate in the celebration of Mass, the priest or deacon invites us to exchange a sign of peace with one another. Remembering Jesus' words, let us exchange with one another some sign of God's peace.

All: *Exchange a sign of peace.*

Closing

Leader: Let us pray together the prayer that Jesus taught.

All: **Our Father . . .**

Chapter 7

Sharing Bread

Gathering

All: ***Gather in the prayer area.***

Leader: Jesus promised that whenever we gather in his name, he is in our midst. With this in mind, we begin with the Sign of the Cross.

All: ***All sign themselves.***

Leader: Let us bow our heads and remember that the Lord is with us in this moment of prayer. *(Pause.)*

Heavenly Father, by sharing in the Eucharist which your Son commanded us to offer as his memorial, may we become, with him, an everlasting gift to you. We ask this through Jesus Christ our Lord, who lives and reigns for ever and ever.

All: **Amen.**

Scripture Reading

Leader: The ancient roots of our celebration of the Eucharist are found in the Jewish Passover—God leading the Israelites out of slavery in Egypt. The celebration of the Passover commemorates that liberation. The unleavened bread, the "bread of affliction," that is eaten every year at Passover is a reminder of the haste with which the Israelites had to flee from Pharaoh. Listen now to these words of Moses, as he commands the Israelites to commemorate faithfully how God delivered them.

Reader: A reading from the Book of Deuteronomy.
Proclaim Deuteronomy 16:1–3.
Conclude by saying,
The word of the Lord.

All: **Thanks be to God.**

Prayer of Intercession

Leader: Let us remember in prayer the children of God whose daily bread is a "bread of affliction."

Reader: For those who suffer physical agony, either from the pain of illness or from torture, let us pray to the Lord:

All: **Lord, hear our prayer.**

Reader: For those whose homes and livelihood have been lost due to the ravages of war or natural disasters, let us pray to the Lord:

All: **Lord, hear our prayer.**

Reader: For the terminally ill, for children dying of AIDS, and for those who grieve the loss of loved ones, let us pray to the Lord:

All: **Lord, hear our prayer.**

Reader: For candidates throughout the world who are preparing for the Sacrament of Confirmation, and for their sponsors and their families, let us pray to the Lord:

All: **Lord, hear our prayer.**

Reader: Let us now pray in silence for our personal intentions. *(Pause.)*
Let us pray to the Lord:

All: **Lord, hear our prayer.**

Ritual Action: Sharing Bread

Leader: Sharing the unleavened "bread of affliction" at Passover reminds the Jewish people to this day of the sufferings of God's people under all of the "pharaohs" of this world. The Eucharist continues to use unleavened bread, but it is for us a memorial of the Passover of Jesus—the passage he made through suffering and death into life without end. We will now share with one another a bite of unleavened bread. I invite you to think of it as "bread of affliction" that symbolizes all of those who suffer in this world from the slavery of sin, violence, poverty, despair, and any other burden. We share it in solidarity with all people for whom Jesus suffered and died. I invite you now to be still for a moment and to think of those with whom you wish to share this bread.

All: *Share the unleavened bread.*

Closing

Leader: Let us pray together the prayer that Jesus taught.

All: **Our Father . . .**

Chapter 8

Spreading the Good News

Gathering

All: ***Gather in the prayer area.***

Leader: Jesus promised that whenever we gather in his name, he is in our midst. With this in mind, we pray the Sign of the Cross.

All: ***All sign themselves.***

Leader: Let us bow our heads and remember that the Lord is with us in this moment of prayer. *(Pause.)*

God our Father, you sent your Son into the world to be its true light. Pour out the Holy Spirit to awaken our faith and help us share the Gospel with others. We ask this through our Lord Jesus Christ, your Son, who lives and reigns with you and the Holy Spirit, one God, for ever and ever.

All: **Amen.**

Scripture Reading

Leader: The Holy Spirit is present with the Church, guiding her to proclaim the Gospel in word and deed with the same fearless power as Jesus did. Listen to these passages from the Acts of the Apostles and pay attention to how Saint Luke shows that the bold preaching of the Apostles reveals the Holy Spirit at work in them.

Reader 1: *Proclaim Acts of the Apostles 1:6–8. Pause briefly before handing the Bible to the next reader.*

Reader 2: *Proclaim Acts of the Apostles 2:38–41. Pause briefly before handing the Bible to the next reader.*

Reader 3: *Proclaim Acts of the Apostles 3:2–10. Pause briefly before handing the Bible to the next reader.*

Reader 4: *Proclaim Acts of the Apostles 5:27–32.*

Ritual Action: Offering a Blessing

Leader: The Holy Spirit gave the Apostles the courage to be fearless, bold, and public witnesses to their faith in Jesus. That same Holy Spirit has been given to us at Baptism. We too are called to offer public witness to our faith in Jesus. Several members of our group have been asked and have agreed to offer a short witness to how their faith in Jesus has grown stronger during the time of their preparation for Confirmation.

Let us raise our hands in support and ask for God's blessing on them.

All: ***Raise your hands and echo this prayer after the leader.***

Leader: May you be blessed with God's grace as you share your faith with others.

Prayer of Intercession

Leader: Let us remember in prayer all the baptized, who are called to proclaim the Gospel wherever they are.

Reader: For those in our midst who diligently fulfill Jesus' command to make disciples of all people, let us pray to the Lord:

All: **Lord, hear our prayer.**

Reader: For those who suffer because of their efforts to live the Gospel, let us pray to the Lord:

All: **Lord, hear our prayer.**

Reader: For those who embrace poverty, live a simple life, leave their families and friends, and travel to live and preach the Gospel, let us pray to the Lord:

All: **Lord, hear our prayer.**

Reader: For all the newly confirmed, their sponsors, and their families that they generously respond to the dismissal at Mass and bear witness to Christ wherever they are, let us pray to the Lord:

All: **Lord, hear our prayer.**

Reader: Let us now pray in silence for our personal intentions. *(Pause.)* Let us pray to the Lord:

All: **Lord, hear our prayer.**

Closing

Leader: Let us pray together the prayer that Jesus taught.

All: **Our Father . . .**

Celebrating Confirmation

The rite for the celebration of the Sacrament of Confirmation usually takes place at Mass "in order that the fundamental connection of this sacrament with all of Christian initiation may stand out in a clearer light. Christian initiation reaches its culmination in the communion of the Body and Blood of Christ. The newly confirmed therefore participate in the eucharist, which completes their Christian initiation" (Introduction 13). The bishop is the ordinary minister of Confirmation. For pastoral reasons he may delegate a priest to administer the sacrament.

SACRAMENT OF CONFIRMATION

Presentation of the Candidates

After the Gospel the bishop and the priests who will be ministers of the sacrament with him take their seats. The pastor or another priest, deacon, or catechist presents the candidates for confirmation, according to the custom of the region. If possible, each candidate is called by name and comes individually to the sanctuary. If the candidates are children, they are accompanied by one of their sponsors or parents and stand before the celebrant.

Homily or Instruction

The bishop then gives a brief homily.

Renewal of Baptismal Promises

After the homily the candidates stand and the bishop questions them:

BISHOP: Do you reject Satan and all his works and all his empty promises?

CANDIDATES: I do.

BISHOP: Do you believe in God the Father almighty, creator of heaven and earth?

CANDIDATES: I do.

BISHOP: Do you believe in Jesus Christ, his only Son, our Lord, who was born of the Virgin Mary, was crucified, died, and was buried, rose from the dead, and is now seated at the right hand of the Father?

CANDIDATES: I do.

BISHOP: Do you believe in the Holy Spirit, the Lord, the giver of life, who came upon the apostles at Pentecost and today is given to you sacramentally in confirmation?

CANDIDATES: I do.

BISHOP: Do you believe in the holy catholic Church, the communion of saints, the forgiveness of sins, the resurrection of the body, and life everlasting?

CANDIDATES: I do.

BISHOP: This is our faith. This is the faith of the Church. We are proud to profess it in Christ Jesus our Lord.

ALL PRESENT: **Amen.**

Give them the spirit of wisdom
and understanding,
the spirit of right judgment and
courage,
the spirit of knowledge and
reverence.
Fill them with the spirit of wonder
and awe in your presence.
We ask this through Christ
our Lord.

ALL: **Amen.**

The Laying On of Hands

"The laying of hands on the candidates by the bishop and the concelebrating priests represents the biblical gesture by which the gift of the Holy Spirit is invoked" (Introduction 9). The concelebrating priests stand near the bishop. He faces the people and with hands joined, sings or says:

BISHOP: My dear friends:
in baptism God our Father gave
the new birth of eternal life
to his chosen sons and daughters.
Let us pray to our Father
that he will pour out the Holy Spirit
to strengthen his sons and
daughters with his gifts
and anoint them to be more like
Christ the Son of God.

All pray in silence for a short time.

The bishop and the priests who will administer the sacrament with him lay hands upon all the candidates (by extending their hands over them). The bishop alone sings or says:

All-powerful God, Father of our
Lord Jesus Christ,
by water and the Holy Spirit
you freed your sons and daughters
from sin
and gave them new life.
Send your Holy Spirit upon them
to be their Helper and Guide.

The Anointing of Chrism

"The anointing with chrism and the accompanying words express clearly the effect of the giving of the Holy Spirit. Signed with the perfumed oil, the baptized receive the indelible character, the seal of the Lord, together with the gift of the Holy Spirit that conforms them more closely to Christ and gives them the grace of spreading 'the sweet odor of Christ'" (Introduction 9). The deacon brings the Chrism to the bishop. Each candidate goes to the bishop, or the bishop may go to the individual candidates. The one who presented the candidate places his right hand on the latter's shoulder and gives the candidate's name to the bishop; or the candidate may give his own name.

BISHOP: *Dips his right thumb in the Chrism and makes the sign of the cross on the forehead of the one to be confirmed, as he says:*
(Name), be sealed with the gift
of the Holy Spirit.

NEWLY CONFIRMED: **Amen.**

BISHOP: Peace be with you.

NEWLY CONFIRMED: **And also with you.**

General Intercession

The general intercessions, or prayer of the faithful, follow.

CONCLUDING RITES

Blessing

Instead of the usual blessing at the end of Mass, the following blessing or prayer over the people is used.

BISHOP: God our Father
made you his children by water
and the Holy Spirit:
may he bless you
and watch over you with his
fatherly love.

ALL: **Amen.**

BISHOP: Jesus Christ the Son of God
promised that the Spirit of truth
would be with his Church for ever:
may he bless you and give you
courage
in professing the true faith.

ALL: **Amen.**

BISHOP: The Holy Spirit
came down upon the disciples
and set their hearts on fire with love:
may he bless you,
keep you one in faith and love,
and bring you to the joy of God's
kingdom.

ALL: **Amen.**

BISHOP: May almighty God bless you,
the Father, and the Son, and the
Holy Spirit.

ALL: **Amen.**

Prayer Over the People

Instead of the preceding blessing, the prayer over the people may be used.

DEACON OR OTHER MINISTER: Bow your heads and pray for God's blessing.

BISHOP: *Extends his hands over the people*
and sings or says:
God our Father,
complete the work you have begun
and keep the gifts of your
Holy Spirit active in the hearts
of your people. Make them ready
to live his Gospel and eager
to do his will. May they never
be ashamed to proclaim to all the
world Christ crucified living and
reigning for ever and ever.

ALL: **Amen.**

BISHOP: And may the blessing of
almighty God
the Father, and the Son, and the
Holy Spirit
come upon you and remain with
you for ever.

ALL: **Amen.**

Catholic Prayers and Practices

Sign of the Cross

In the name of the Father,
and of the Son,
and of the Holy Spirit. Amen.

Signum Crucis

In nómine Patris,
et Filii,
et Spíritu Sancti. Amen.

Glory Prayer

Glory to the Father,
and to the Son,
and to the Holy Spirit:
as it was in the beginning, is now,
and will be for ever. Amen.

Gloria Patri

Glória Patri
et Filio
et Spirítui Sancto.
Sicut erat in princípio,
et nunc et semper
et in sǽcula sæculórum. Amen.

Lord's Prayer

Our Father, who art in heaven,
hallowed be thy name;
thy kingdom come;
thy will be done on earth
as it is in heaven.
Give us this day our daily bread;
and forgive us our trespasses
as we forgive those who trespass
against us;
and lead us not into temptation,
but deliver us from evil. Amen.

Pater Noster

Pater noster, qui es in cælis:
sanctificétur nomen tuum;
advéniat regnum tuum;
fiat volúntas tua, sicut in cælo, et in terra.
Panem nostrum cotidiánum
da nobis hódie;
et dimítte nobis débita nostra,
sicut et nos dimíttimus debitóribus nostris;
et ne nos indúcas in tentatiónem;
sed líbera nos a malo. Amen.

Hail Mary

Hail Mary, full of grace,
the Lord is with you!
Blessed are you among women,
and blessed is the fruit
of your womb, Jesus.
Holy Mary, Mother of God,
pray for us sinners,
now and at the hour of our death. Amen.

Ave, Maria

Ave, María, grátia plena,
Dóminus tecum.
Benedícta tu in muliéribus,
et benedíctus fructus ventris tui, Jesus.
Sancta María, Mater Dei,
ora pro nobis peccatóribus,
nunc et in hora mortis nostræ. Amen.

The four prayers on this page are in English and in Latin.
Latin is the universal language of the Roman Catholic Church.

Prayer to the Holy Spirit

Come, Holy Spirit, fill the hearts
of your faithful.
And kindle in them the
fire of your love.
Send forth your Spirit and
they shall be created.
And you will renew the
face of the earth.

Act of Contrition

My God,
I am sorry for my sins with all my heart.
In choosing to do wrong
and failing to do good,
I have sinned against you
whom I should love above all things.
I firmly intend, with your help,
to do penance,
to sin no more,
and to avoid whatever leads me to sin.
Our Savior Jesus Christ
suffered and died for us.
In his name, my God, have mercy.

Nicene Creed

We believe in one God,
the Father, the Almighty,
maker of heaven and earth,
of all that is, seen and unseen.

We believe in one Lord, Jesus Christ,
the only Son of God,
eternally begotten of the Father,
God from God, Light from Light,
true God from true God,
begotten, not made, one in Being
with the Father.
Through him all things were made.
For us men and for our salvation
he came down from heaven:

by the power of the Holy Spirit
he was born of the Virgin Mary, and
became man.

For our sake he was crucified under
Pontius Pilate;
he suffered, died, and was buried.
On the third day he rose again
in fulfillment of the Scriptures;
he ascended into heaven
and is seated at the right hand
of the Father.
He will come again in glory to judge
the living and the dead,
and his kingdom will have no end.

We believe in the Holy Spirit, the Lord,
the giver of life,
who proceeds from the Father
and the Son.
With the Father and the Son he is
worshiped and glorified.

He has spoken through the Prophets.
We believe in one holy catholic and
apostolic Church.
We acknowledge one baptism for the
forgiveness of sins.
We look for the resurrection of the dead,
and the life of the world to come. Amen.

Act of Faith

My God, I firmly believe that you are one God
in three divine Persons, Father, Son, and Holy
Spirit; I believe that your divine Son became
man and died for our sins, and that he will
come to judge the living and the dead. Amen.

Act of Hope

My God, relying on your infinite goodness
and promises, I hope to obtain pardon of
my sins, the help of your grace, and life
everlasting, through the merits of Jesus
Christ, my Lord and Redeemer. Amen.

Act of Love

My God, I love you above all things, with my
whole heart and soul, because you are all
good and worthy of all my love. I love my
neighbor as myself for the love of you. I
forgive all who have injured me and I ask
pardon of all whom I have injured. Amen.

Rosary

Catholics pray the Rosary to honor Mary and remember the important events in the life of Jesus and Mary. We begin praying the Rosary by praying the Apostles' Creed, the Lord's Prayer, and three Hail Marys. Each mystery of the Rosary is prayed by praying the Lord's Prayer once, the Hail Mary ten times, and the Glory Prayer once. When we have finished the last mystery, we pray the Hail, Holy Queen.

Joyful Mysteries

1. The Annunciation
2. The Visitation
3. The Nativity
4. The Presentation
5. The Finding of Jesus in the Temple

Mysteries of Light

1. The Baptism of Jesus in the Jordan River
2. The Miracle at the Wedding at Cana
3. The Proclamation of the Kingdom of God
4. The Transfiguration of Jesus
5. The Institution of the Eucharist

Sorrowful Mysteries

1. The Agony in the Garden
2. The Scourging at the Pillar
3. The Crowning with Thorns
4. The Carrying of the Cross
5. The Crucifixion

Glorious Mysteries

1. The Resurrection
2. The Ascension
3. The Coming of the Holy Spirit
4. The Assumption of Mary
5. The Coronation of Mary

Hail, Holy Queen

Hail, holy Queen, mother of mercy,
hail, our life, our sweetness,
    and our hope.
To you we cry, the children of Eve;
to you we send up our sighs,
mourning and weeping
    in this land of exile.
Turn, then, most gracious advocate,
your eyes of mercy toward us;
lead us home at last
and show us the blessed fruit
    of your womb, Jesus:
O clement, O loving, O sweet Virgin Mary.

Memorare

Remember, most loving Virgin Mary,
never was it heard
that anyone who turned to you for help
was left unaided.

Inspired by this confidence,
though burdened by my sins,
I run to your protection,
for you are my mother.

Mother of the Word of God,
do not despise my words of pleading
but be merciful and hear my prayer. Amen.

The Ten Commandments

1. I am the Lord your God: you shall not have strange gods before me.
2. You shall not take the name of the LORD your God in vain.
3. Remember to keep holy the LORD's Day.
4. Honor your father and your mother.
5. You shall not kill.
6. You shall not commit adultery.
7. You shall not steal.
8. You shall not bear false witness against your neighbor.
9. You shall not covet your neighbor's wife.
10. You shall not covet your neighbor's goods.

The Beatitudes

"Blessed are the poor in spirit,
    for theirs is the kingdom of heaven.
Blessed are they who mourn,
    for they will be comforted.
Blessed are the meek,
    for they will inherit the land.
Blessed are they who hunger
        and thirst for righteousness,
    for they will be satisfied.
Blessed are the merciful,
    for they will be shown mercy.
Blessed are the clean of heart,
    for they will see God.
Blessed are the peacemakers,
    for they will be called children of God.
Blessed are they who are persecuted for
        the sake of righteousness,
    for theirs is the kingdom of heaven.

"Blessed are you when they insult you and persecute you and utter every kind of evil against you [falsely] because of me. Rejoice and be glad, for your reward will be great in heaven."   MATTHEW 5:3–12

The Great Commandment

"You shall love the Lord,
your God, with all your
heart, with all your soul,
and with all your mind. . . .
You shall love your neighbor as yourself."
                    MATTHEW 22:37, 39

Corporal Works of Mercy

Feed people who are hungry.
Give drink to people who are thirsty.
Clothe people who need clothes.
Visit prisoners.
Shelter people who are homeless.
Visit people who are sick.
Bury people who have died.

Spiritual Works of Mercy

Help people who sin.
Teach people who are ignorant.
Give advice to people who have doubts.
Comfort people who suffer.
Be patient with other people.
Forgive people who hurt you.
Pray for people who are alive and
        for those who have died.

Gifts of the Holy Spirit

Wisdom
Understanding
Right judgment (Counsel)
Courage (Fortitude)
Knowledge
Reverence (Piety)
Wonder and awe (Fear of the Lord)

Fruits of the Holy Spirit

charity	kindness	faithfulness
joy	goodness	modesty
peace	generosity	self-control
patience	gentleness	chastity

The Sacrament of Reconciliation

Individual Rite
Greeting
Scripture Reading
Confession of Sins and Acceptance
  of Penance
Act of Contrition
Absolution
Closing Prayer

Communal Rite
Greeting
Scripture Reading
Homily
Examination of Conscience with a litany
  of contrition and the Lord's Prayer
Individual Confession and Absolution
Closing Prayer

Act of Contrition
My God,
I am sorry for my sins
  with all my heart.
In choosing to do wrong
and failing to do good,
I have sinned against you
whom I should love above all things.
I firmly intend, with your help,
to do penance,
to sin no more,
and to avoid whatever leads me to sin.
Our Savior Jesus Christ
suffered and died for us.
In his name, my God, have mercy.

Basic Principles of the Church's Teaching on Social Justice

The Church's teaching on social justice guides us in living lives of holiness and building a just society. These principles are:

1. All human life is sacred. The basic equality of all people flows from their dignity as human persons and the rights that flow from that dignity.

2. The human person is the principle, the object, and the subject of every social group.

3. The human person has been created by God to belong to and to participate in a family and other social communities.

4. Respect for the rights of people flows from their dignity as persons. Society and all social organizations must promote virtue and protect human life and human rights and guarantee the conditions that promote the exercise of freedom.

5. Political communities and public authority are based on human nature. They belong to an order established by God.

6. All human authority must be used for the common good of society.

7. The common good of society consists of respect for and promotion of the fundamental rights of the human person; the just development of material and spiritual goods of society; and the peace and safety of all people.

8. We need to work to eliminate the sinful inequalities that exist between peoples and for the improvement of the living conditions of people. The needs of the poor and vulnerable have a priority.

9. We are one human and global family. We are to share our spiritual blessings, even more than our material blessings.

Based on the *Catechism of the Catholic Church*

Key Teachings of the Catholic Church*

THE MYSTERY OF GOD

DIVINE REVELATION

Who am I?
Every human person has been created by God to live in friendship with him both here on earth and forever in heaven.

How do we know this about ourselves?
We know this because every human person desires to know and love God as well as desires that God know and love them. We also know this because God told us this about ourselves and about him.

How did God tell us?
First of all God tells us this through creation, which is the work of God; creation reflects the goodness and beauty of the Creator and tells us about God the Creator. Secondly, God came to us and told us, or revealed this about himself. He revealed this most fully by sending his Son, Jesus Christ, who became one of us and lived among us.

What is faith?
Faith is a supernatural gift from God that enables us to come to know God and all that he has revealed, and to respond to God with our whole heart and mind.

What is a mystery of faith?
The word *mystery* describes the fact that we can never fully comprehend or fully grasp God and his loving plan for us. We only know who God is and his plan for us through Divine Revelation.

What is Divine Revelation?
Divine Revelation is God's free gift of making himself known to us and giving himself to us by gradually communicating in deeds and words his own mystery and his divine plan for humanity. God reveals himself so that we can live in communion with him and with one another forever.

What is Sacred Tradition?
The word *tradition* comes from a Latin word meaning "to pass on." Sacred Tradition is the passing on of Divine Revelation by the Church through the power and guidance of the Holy Spirit.

What is the deposit of faith?
The deposit of faith is the source of faith that we draw from in order to pass on God's Revelation. The deposit of faith is the unity of Sacred Scripture and Sacred Tradition handed on by the Church from the time of the Apostles.

What is the Magisterium?
The Magisterium is the teaching authority and teaching office of the Church. Guided by the Holy Spirit, the Church has the responsibility to authentically and accurately interpret the Word of God, both in Sacred Scripture and in Sacred Tradition. She does this to assure that her understanding of Revelation is faithful to the teaching of the Apostles.

What is a dogma of faith?
A dogma of faith is a truth taught by the Church as revealed by God and to which we are called to give our assent of mind and heart.

SACRED SCRIPTURE

What is Sacred Scripture?
The words *sacred scripture* come from two Latin words meaning "holy writings." Sacred Scripture is the collection of all the writings God has inspired authors to write in his name.

What is the Bible?
The word *bible* comes from a Greek word meaning "book." The Bible is the collection of the forty-six books of the Old Testament and the twenty-seven books of the New Testament named by the Church as all the writings God has inspired human authors to write in his name.

What is the canon of Scripture?
The word *canon* comes from a Greek word meaning "measuring rod," or standard by which something is judged. The canon of Scripture is the list of books that the Catholic Church has identified and teaches to be the inspired Word of God.

What is biblical inspiration?
Biblical inspiration is a term that describes the Holy Spirit guiding the human writers of Sacred Scripture so that they faithfully and accurately communicate the Word of God.

What is the Old Testament?
The Old Testament is the first main part of the Bible. It is the forty-six books inspired by the Holy Spirit, written before the birth of Jesus and centered on the Covenant between God and his people, Israel, and the promise of the Messiah or Savior. The Old Testament is divided into the Torah/Pentateuch, historical books, wisdom literature, and writings of the prophets.

What is the Torah?

The Torah is the Law of God that was revealed to Moses. The written Torah is found in the first five books of the Old Testament, which are called the "Torah" and the "Pentateuch."

What is the Pentateuch?

The word *pentateuch* means "five containers." The Pentateuch is the first five books of the Old Testament, namely Genesis, Exodus, Leviticus, Numbers, and Deuteronomy.

What is the Covenant?

The Covenant is the solemn agreement of fidelity that God and the people of God freely entered into. It was renewed and fulfilled in Jesus Christ, the new and everlasting Covenant.

What are the historical books of the Old Testament?

The historical books tell about the fidelity and infidelity of God's people to the Covenant and about the consequences of those choices.

What are the Wisdom writings of the Old Testament?

The Wisdom writings are the seven books of the Old Testament that contain inspired practical advice and common-sense guidelines for living the Covenant and the Law of God. They are the Book of Job, Book of Psalms, Book of Ecclesiastes, Book of Wisdom, Book of Proverbs, Book of Sirach (Ecclesiasticus), and Song of Songs.

What are the writings of the prophets in the Old Testament?

The word *prophet* comes from a Greek word meaning "those who speak before others." The biblical prophets were those people God has chosen to speak in his name. The writings of the prophets are the eighteen books of the Old Testament that contain the message of the prophets to God's people. They remind God's people of God's unending fidelity to them and of their responsibility to be faithful to the Covenant.

What is the New Testament?

The New Testament is the second main part of the Bible. It is the twenty-seven books inspired by the Holy Spirit and written in apostolic times that center on Jesus Christ and his saving work among us. The main parts of the New Testament are the Gospels, the Acts of the Apostles, the twenty-one New Testament epistles, or letters, and the Book of Revelation.

What are the Gospels?

The word *gospel* comes from a Greek word meaning "good news." The Gospel is the Good News of God's loving plan of Salvation, revealed in the Passion, death, Resurrection, and Ascension of Jesus Christ. The Gospels are the four written accounts of Matthew, Mark, Luke, and John. The four Gospels occupy a central place in Sacred Scripture because Jesus Christ is their center.

What is an epistle?

The word *epistle* comes from a Greek word meaning "message or letter." Epistles are a longer, more formal type of letter. Some of the letters in the New Testament are epistles.

What are the Pauline epistles and letters?

The Pauline epistles and letters are the thirteen letters in the New Testament attributed to Saint Paul the Apostle.

What are the Catholic Letters?

The Catholic Letters are the seven New Testament letters that bear the names of the Apostles John, Peter, Jude, and James, and which were written to the universal Church rather than to a particular Church community.

THE HOLY TRINITY

Who is the Mystery of the Holy Trinity?

The Holy Trinity is the mystery of one God in three Persons—God the Father, God the Son, God the Holy Spirit. It is the central mystery of the Christian faith.

Who is God the Father?

God the Father is the first Person of the Holy Trinity.

Who is God the Son?

God the Son is Jesus Christ, the second Person of the Holy Trinity. He is the only begotten Son of the Father who took on flesh and became one of us without giving up his divinity.

Who is God the Holy Spirit?

God the Holy Spirit is the third Person of the Holy Trinity, who proceeds from the Father and Son. He is the Advocate, or Paraclete, sent to us by the Father in the name of his Son, Jesus.

What are the divine missions, or the works of God?

The divine missions are the particular works of God attributed to each of the three Persons of the Holy Trinity. The work of creation is attributed to the Father, the work of Salvation is attributed to the Son, and the work of sanctification, or our holiness, is attributed to the Holy Spirit.

DIVINE WORK OF CREATION

What is the divine work of creation?

Creation is the work of God bringing into existence everything and everyone, seen and unseen, out of love and without any help.

Who are angels?

Angels are spiritual creatures who do not have bodies as humans do. Angels give glory to God without ceasing and sometimes serve God by bringing his message to people.

Who is the human person?

"The dignity of the human person is in their creation in the image and likeness of God." (See Genesis 1:27.) This dignity is fulfilled in the vocation to a life of happiness with God.

What is the soul?

Our soul is the spiritual part of who we are. It is immortal; it never dies. Our soul is our innermost being, that which bears the imprint of the image of God.

What is the intellect?

Our intellect is an essential power of our soul. It is the power to know God, ourselves, and others; it is the power to understand the order of things established by God.

What is free will?

Free will is an essential quality of the soul. It is the God-given ability and power to recognize him as part of our lives and to choose to center our lives around him as well as to choose between good and evil. By free will, the human person is capable of directing himself toward his true good, namely, life in communion with God.

What is Original Sin?

Original sin is the sin of Adam and Eve by which they choose evil over obedience to God and by doing so lost the state of original holiness for themselves for all their descendants. As a result of original sin, death, sin, and suffering entered the world.

JESUS CHRIST, THE INCARNATE SON OF GOD

What is the Annunciation?

The Annunciation is the announcement by the angel Gabriel to Mary that she was chosen by God to become the Mother of Jesus, the Son of God, by the power of the Holy Spirit.

What is the Incarnation?

The word *incarnation* comes from a Latin word meaning "take on flesh." The term Incarnation is the fact that the Son of God, the second Person of the Holy Trinity, truly became human while remaining truly God. Jesus Christ is true God and true man.

What is the Paschal Mystery?

The Paschal Mystery is the saving events of the Passion, death, Resurrection, and glorious Ascension of Jesus Christ; the passing over of Jesus from death into a new and glorious life; the name we give to God's plan of Salvation in Jesus Christ.

What is Salvation?

The word *salvation* comes from a Latin word meaning "to save." Salvation is the saving, or deliverance, of humanity from the power of sin and death through Jesus Christ "who died for our sins in accordance with the scriptures" (1 Corinthians 15:3). All Salvation comes from Christ the Head through the Church, which is his Body.

What is the Resurrection?

The Resurrection is the historical fact of Jesus being raised from the dead to a new glorified life after his death on the cross and burial in the tomb.

What is the Ascension

The Ascension is the return of the Risen Christ in glory to his Father, to the world of the divine.

What is the Second Coming of Christ?

The Second Coming of Christ is the return of Christ in glory at the end of time to judge the living and the dead; the fulfillment of God's plan in Christ.

What does it mean that Jesus is Lord?

The word *lord* means "master, ruler, a person of authority" and is used in the Old Testament to name God. The designation, or title, "Jesus, the Lord" expresses that Jesus is truly God.

What does it mean that Jesus is the Messiah?

The word *messiah* is a Hebrew term meaning "anointed one." Jesus Christ is the Anointed One, the Messiah, who God promised to send to save people. Jesus is the Savior of the world.

THE MYSTERY OF THE CHURCH

What is the Church?

The word *church* means "convocation, those called together." The Church is the sacrament of Salvation—the sign and instrument of our reconciliation and communion with God the Holy Trinity and with one another. The Church is the Body of Christ, the people God the Father has called together in Jesus Christ through the power of the Holy Spirit.

What is the central work of the Church?

The central work of the Church is to proclaim the Gospel, or Good News, of Jesus Christ and to invite all people to come to know and believe in him and to live in communion with him. We call this work of the Church "evangelization," a word that comes from a Greek word that means "to tell good news."

What is the Body of Christ?

The Body of Christ is an image for the Church used by Saint Paul the Apostle that teaches that all the members of the Church are one in Christ, who is the Head of the Church, and that all members have a unique and vital work in the Church.

Who are the People of God?

The new People of God are those the Father has chosen and gathered in Christ, the Incarnate Son of God, the Church. All people are invited to belong to the People of God and to live as one family of God.

What is the Temple of the Holy Spirit?

The Temple of the Holy Spirit is a New Testament image used to describe the indwelling of the Holy Spirit in the Church and within the hearts of the faithful.

What is the Communion of Saints?

The Communion of Saints is the communion of holy things and holy people that make up the Church. It is the communion, or unity, of all the faithful, those living on earth, those being purified after death, and those enjoying life everlasting and eternal happiness with God, the angels, and Mary and all the saints.

What are the Marks of the Church?

The Marks of the Church are the four attributes and essential characteristics of the Church and her mission, namely, one, holy, catholic, and apostolic.

Who are the Apostles?

The word *apostle* comes from a Greek word meaning "to send away." The Apostles were those disciples chosen and sent by Jesus to preach the Gospel and to make disciples of all people.

Who are the "Twelve"?

The "Twelve" is the term that identifies the Apostles chosen by Jesus before his death and Resurrection. "The names of the twelve apostles are these: first, Simon called Peter, and his brother Andrew; James, the son of Zebedee, and his brother John; Philip and Bartholomew, Thomas and Matthew the tax collector; James the son of Alphaeus, and Thaddaeus; Simon the Cananean, and Judas Iscariot who betrayed him" (Matthew 10:2–4). The Apostles Matthias and Paul were chosen after Jesus' Ascension.

What is Pentecost?

Pentecost is the coming of the Holy Spirit upon the Church as promised by Jesus; it marks the beginning of the work of the Church.

Who are the ordained ministers of the Church?

The ordained ministers of the Church are those baptized men who are consecrated in the Sacrament of Holy Orders to serve the whole Church. Bishops, priests, and deacons are the ordained ministers of the Church and make up the clergy.

How do the pope and other bishops guide the Church in her work?

Christ, the Head of the Church, governs the Church through the pope and the college of bishops in communion with him. The pope is the bishop of Rome and the successor of Saint Peter the Apostle. The pope, the Vicar of Christ, is the visible foundation of the unity of the whole Church. The other bishops are the successors of the other Apostles and are the visible foundation of their own particular Churches. The Holy Spirit guides the pope alone, and the college of bishops working together with the pope, to teach the faith and moral doctrine without error. This grace of the Holy Spirit is called *infallibility*.

What is the consecrated life?

The consecrated life is a state of life for those baptized who promise or vow to live the Gospel by means of professing the evangelical counsels of poverty, chastity, and obedience, in a way of life approved by the Church. The consecrated life is also known as the religious life.

Who are the laity?

The laity (or laypeople) are all the baptized who have not received the Sacrament of Holy Orders nor have promised or vowed to live the consecrated life. They are called to be witnesses to Christ at the very heart of the human community.

THE BLESSED VIRGIN MARY

What is Mary's role in God's loving plan for humanity?

Mary has a unique role in God's plan of Salvation for humanity. For this reason she was full of grace from the first moment of her conception, or existence. God chose Mary to be the mother of the Incarnate Son of God, Jesus Christ, who is truly God and truly man. Mary is the Mother of God, the Mother of Christ, and the Mother of the Church. She is the greatest saint of the Church.

What is the Immaculate Conception?

The Immaculate Conception is the unique grace given to Mary that totally preserved her from the stain of all sin from the very first moment of her existence, or conception, in her mother's womb and throughout her life.

What is the perpetual virginity of Mary?

The perpetual virginity of Mary is a term that described the fact that Mary was always a virgin. She was virgin before the conception of Jesus, during his birth, and remained a virgin after the birth of Jesus her whole life.

What is the Assumption of Mary?

At the end of her life on earth, the Blessed Virgin Mary was taken body and soul into heaven, where she shares in the glory of her Son's Resurrection. Mary, the Mother of the Church, hears our prayers and intercedes for us with her Son. She is an image of the heavenly glory in which we all hope to share when Christ, her Son, comes again in glory.

LIFE EVERLASTING

What is eternal life?

Eternal life is life after death. At death the soul is separated from the body. In the Apostles' Creed we profess faith in "the life everlasting." In the Nicene Creed we profess faith in "the life of the world to come."

What is the particular judgment?

The particular judgment is the assignment given to our souls at the moment of our death to our final destiny based on what we have done in our lives.

What is the Last Judgment?

The Last Judgment is the judgment at which all the humans will appear in their own bodies and give an account of their deeds. At the Last Judgment Christ will show his identity with the least of his brothers and sisters.

What is the beatific vision?

The beatific vision is seeing God face-to-face in heavenly glory.

What is heaven?

Heaven is eternal life and communion with the Holy Trinity. It is the supreme state of happiness of living with God forever for which he created us.

What is the Kingdom of God?

The Kingdom of God, or Kingdom of Heaven, is the image used by Jesus to describe all people and creation living in communion with God. The Kingdom of God will be fully realized when Christ comes again in glory at the end of time.

What is purgatory?

Purgatory is the opportunity after death to purify and strengthen our love for God before we enter heaven.

What is hell?

Hell is the immediate and everlasting separation from God and the saints.

CELEBRATION OF THE CHRISTIAN LIFE AND MYSTERY

LITURGY AND WORSHIP

What is worship?

Worship is the adoration and honor given to God. The Church worships God publicly in the celebration of the liturgy.

What is the liturgy of the Church?

The liturgy is the Church's worship of God. It is the work of the whole Christ, Head and Body. In the liturgy the mystery of Salvation in Christ is made present by the power of the Holy Spirit.

What is the liturgical year?

The liturgical year is the cycle of seasons and great feasts that make up the Church year of worship. The main seasons of the Church year are Advent, Christmas, Lent, Easter Triduum, Easter, and Ordinary Time.

THE SACRAMENTS

What are the sacraments?

The sacraments are seven signs of God's love and the main liturgical actions of the Church through which the faithful are made sharers in the Paschal Mystery of Christ. The sacraments are effective signs of grace, instituted by Christ and entrusted to the Church, by which divine life is shared with us.

What are the Sacraments of Christian Initiation?

The Sacraments of Christian Initiation are Baptism, Confirmation, and Eucharist. These three sacraments are the foundation of every Christian life. "Baptism is the beginning of new life in Christ; Confirmation is its strengthening; the Eucharist nourishes the faithful for their transformation into Christ."

What is the Sacrament of Baptism?

Through Baptism we are reborn into new life in Christ. We are joined to Jesus Christ, become members of the Church, and are reborn as God's children. We receive the gift of the Holy Spirit, and original sin and our personal sins are forgiven. Baptism marks us indelibly and forever as belonging to Christ. Because of this, Baptism can be received only once.

What is the Sacrament of Confirmation?

Confirmation strengthens the graces of Baptism and celebrates the special gift of the Holy Spirit. Confirmation also imprints a spiritual or indelible character on the soul and can be received only once.

What is the Sacrament of the Eucharist?

The Eucharist is the source and summit of the Christian life. In the Eucharist the faithful join with Christ to give thanksgiving, honor, and glory to the Father through the power of the Holy Spirit. Through the power of the Holy Spirit and the words of the priest, the bread and wine become the Body and Blood of Christ.

What is the obligation of the faithful to participate in the Eucharist?

The faithful have the obligation to participate in the Eucharist on Sundays and holy days of obligation. Sunday is the Lord's Day. Sunday, the day of the Lord's Resurrection, is "the foundation and kernel of the whole liturgical year." Regular participation in the Eucharist and receiving Holy Communion is vital to the Christian life. In the Eucharist we receive the Body and Blood of Christ.

What is the Blessed Sacrament?

The Blessed Sacrament is another name for the Eucharist. The term is often used to identify the Eucharist reserved in the tabernacle.

What is the Mass?

The Mass is the main celebration of the Church at which we gather to listen to the Word of God (Liturgy of the Word) and through which we are made sharers in the saving death and Resurrection of Christ and give praise and glory to the Father (Liturgy of the Eucharist).

What are the Sacraments of Healing?

Penance and Anointing of the Sick are the two Sacraments of Healing. Through the power of the Holy Spirit, Christ the Physician's work of Salvation and healing of the members of the Church is continued.

What is the Sacrament of Penance, or Reconciliation?

The Sacrament of Penance is one of the two Sacraments of Healing through which we receive God's forgiveness for the sins we have committed after Baptism.

What is confession?

Confession is the telling of sins to a priest in the Sacrament of Penance. This act of the penitent is an essential element of the Sacrament of Penance. Confession is also another name for the Sacrament of Penance.

What is the seal of confession?

The seal of confession is the obligation of the priest to never reveal to anyone what a penitent has confessed to him.

What is contrition?

Contrition is sorrow for sins that includes the desire and commitment to make reparation for the harm caused by our sin and the purpose of amendment not to sin again. Contrition is an essential element of the Sacrament of Penance.

What is a penance?

A penance is a prayer or act of kindness that shows we are truly sorry for our sins and that helps us repair the damage caused by our sin. Accepting and doing our penance is an essential part of the Sacrament of Penance.

What is absolution?

Absolution is the forgiveness of sins by God through the ministry of the priest.

What is the Sacrament of Anointing of the Sick?

The Sacrament of Anointing of the Sick is one of the two Sacraments of Healing. The grace of this sacrament strengthens our faith and trust in God when we are seriously ill, weakened by old age, or dying. The faithful may receive this sacrament each time they are seriously ill or an illness gets worse.

What is Viaticum?

Viaticum is the Eucharist, or Holy Communion, received as food and strength for a dying person's journey from life on earth through death to eternal life.

What are the Sacraments at the Service of Communion?

Holy Orders and Matrimony are the two Sacraments at the Service of Communion. These sacraments bestow a particular work, or mission, on certain members of the Church to serve to build up the People of God.

What is the Sacrament of Holy Orders?

The Sacrament of Holy Orders is one of the two Sacraments at the Service of Communion. It is the sacrament in which baptized men are consecrated as bishops, priests, or deacons to serve the whole Church in the name and person of Christ.

Who is a bishop?

A bishop is a priest who receives the fullness of the Sacrament of Holy Orders. He is a successor of the Apostles and shepherds a particular church entrusted to him by means of teaching, leading divine worship, and governing the Church as Jesus did.

Who is a priest?

A priest is a baptized man who has received the Sacrament of Holy Orders. Priests are coworkers with their bishops, who have the ministry of "authentically teaching the faith, celebrating divine worship, above all the Eucharist, and guiding their Churches as true pastors."

Who is a deacon?

A deacon is ordained to assist bishops and priests. He is not ordained to the priesthood but to a ministry of service to the Church.

What is the Sacrament of Matrimony?

The Sacrament of Matrimony is one of the two Sacraments at the Service of Communion. In the Sacrament of Matrimony a baptized man and a baptized woman dedicate their lives to the Church and to one another in a lifelong bond of faithful life-giving love. In this sacrament they receive the grace to be a living sign of Christ's love for the Church.

What are the sacramentals of the Church?
Sacramentals are sacred signs instituted by the Church. They include blessings, prayers, and certain objects that prepare us to participate in the sacraments and make us aware of and help us respond to God's loving presence in our lives.

LIFE IN THE SPIRIT

THE MORAL LIFE

Why was the human person created?
The human person was created to give honor and glory to God and to live a life of beatitude with God here on earth and forever in heaven.

What is the Christian moral life?
The baptized have new life in Christ in the Holy Spirit. They respond to the "desire for happiness that God has placed in every human heart" by cooperating with the grace of the Holy Spirit and living the Gospel. "The moral life is a spiritual worship that finds its nourishment in the liturgy and celebration of the sacraments."

What is the way to happiness revealed by Jesus Christ?
Jesus taught that the Great Commandment of loving God above all else and our neighbor as ourselves is the path to happiness. It is the summary and heart of the Commandments and all of God's law.

What are the Ten Commandments?
The Ten Commandments are the laws of the Covenant that God revealed to Moses and the Israelites on Mount Sinai. The Ten Commandments are also known as the Decalogue, or "Ten Words." They are the "privileged expression of the natural law," which is written on the hearts of all people.

What are the Beatitudes?
The Beatitudes are the teachings of Jesus that summarize the path to true happiness, the Kingdom of God, which is living in communion and friendship with God, and with Mary and all the saints. The Beatitudes guide us in living as disciples of Christ by keeping our life focused and centered on God.

What is the New Commandment?
The New Commandment is the commandment of love that Jesus gave his disciples. Jesus said, "I give you a new commandment: love one another. As I have loved you, so you should also love one another" (John 13:34).

What are the Works of Mercy?
The word *mercy* comes from a Hebrew word pointing to God's unconditional love and kindness at work in the world. Human works of mercy are acts of loving kindness by which we reach out to people in their corporal and spiritual needs.

What are the Precepts of the Church?
Precepts of the Church are specific responsibilities that concern the moral and Christian life united with the liturgy and nourished by it.

HOLINESS OF LIFE AND GRACE

What is holiness?
Holiness is the state of living in communion with God. It designates both the presence of God, the Holy One, with us and our faithfulness to him. It is the characteristic of a person who is in right relationship with God, with people, and with creation.

What is grace?
Grace is the gift of God sharing his life and love with us. Categories of grace are sanctifying grace, actual grace, charisms, and sacramental graces.

What is sanctifying grace?
The word *sanctifying* comes from a Latin word meaning "to make holy." Sanctifying grace is a gratuitous gift of God, given by the Holy Spirit, as a remedy for sin and the source of holiness.

What is actual grace?
Actual graces are the God-given divine helps empowering us to live as his adopted daughters and sons.

What are charisms?
Charisms are gifts or graces freely given to individual Christians by the Holy Spirit for the benefit of building up the Church.

What are sacramental graces?
Sacramental graces are the graces of each of the sacraments that help us live out our Christian vocation.

What are the Gifts of the Holy Spirit?
The seven Gifts of the Holy Spirit are graces that strengthen us to live our Baptism, our new life in Christ. They are wisdom, understanding, right judgment (or counsel), courage (or fortitude), knowledge, reverence (or piety), wonder and awe (or fear of the Lord).

What are the Fruits of the Holy Spirit?
The twelve Fruits of the Holy Spirit are visible signs and effects of the Holy Spirit at work in our life. They are charity (love), joy, peace, patience, kindness, goodness, generosity, gentleness, faithfulness, modesty, self-control, and chastity.

THE VIRTUES

What are virtues?
The virtues are spiritual powers or habits or behaviors that help us do what is good. The Catholic Church speaks of theological virtues, moral virtues, and cardinal virtues.

What are the theological virtues?
The theological virtues are the three virtues of faith, hope, and charity (love). These virtues are "gifts from God infused into the souls of the faithful to make them capable of acting as his children and of attaining eternal life" (CCC 1813).

What are the moral virtues?
The moral virtues are "firm attitudes, stable dispositions, habitual perfections of intellect and will that govern our actions, order our passions, and guide our conduct according to reason and faith. They make possible ease, self-mastery, and joy in leading a morally good life" (CCC 1804).

What are the cardinal virtues?
The cardinal virtues are the four moral virtues of prudence, justice, fortitude, and temperance. They are called the cardinal virtues because all of the moral virtues are related to and grouped around them.

MORAL EVIL AND SIN

What is moral evil?
Moral evil is the harm we willingly inflict on one another and on God's good creation.

What is conscience?
The word *conscience* comes from a Latin word meaning "to be conscious of guilt." Conscience is that part of every human person that helps us judge whether a moral act is in accordance or not in accordance with God's law; our conscience moves us to do good and avoid evil.

What is temptation?
Temptation is everything, either within us or outside us, that tries to move us from doing something good that we know we can and should do and to do or say something we know is contrary to the will of God. Temptation is whatever tries to move us away from living a holy life.

What is sin?
Sin is freely and knowingly doing or saying what we know is against the will of God and the Law of God. Sin sets itself against God's love and turns our hearts away from his love. The Church speaks of mortal sin, venial sin, and capital sins.

What is mortal sin?
A mortal sin is a serious, deliberate failure in our love and respect for God, our neighbor, creation, and ourselves. It is knowingly and willingly choosing to do something that is gravely contrary to the Law of God. The effect of mortal sin is the loss of sanctifying grace and, if unrepented, mortal sin brings eternal death.

What are venial sins?
Venial sins are sins that are less serious than a mortal sin. They weaken our love for God and for one another and diminish our holiness.

What are capital sins?
Capital sins are sins that are at the root of other sins. The seven capital sins are false pride, avarice, envy, anger, gluttony, lust, and sloth.

CHRISTIAN PRAYER

What is prayer?
Prayer is conversation with God. It is talking and listening to him, raising our minds and hearts to God the Father, Son, and Holy Spirit.

What is the prayer of all Christians?
The Lord's Prayer, or Our Father, is the prayer of all Christians. It is the prayer Jesus taught his disciples and gave to the Church. The Lord's Prayer is "a summary of the whole Gospel." Praying the Lord's Prayer "brings us into communion with the Father and his Son, Jesus Christ" and develops "in us the will to become like [Jesus] and to place our trust in the Father as he did."

What are the traditional expressions of prayer?
The traditional expressions of prayer are vocal prayer, the prayer of meditation, and the prayer of contemplation.

What is vocal prayer?
Vocal prayer is spoken prayer; prayer using words said aloud or in the quiet of one's heart.

What is the prayer of meditation?
Meditation is a form of prayer in which we use our minds, hearts, imaginations, emotions, and desires to understand and follow what the Lord is asking us to do.

What is the prayer of contemplation?
Contemplation is a form of prayer that is simply being with God.

What are the traditional forms of prayer?
The traditional forms of prayer are the prayer of adoration and blessing, the prayer of thanksgiving, the prayer of praise, the prayer of petition, and the prayer of intercession.

What are devotions?
Devotions are part of the prayer life of the Church and of the baptized. They are acts of communal or individual prayer that surround and arise out of the celebration of the liturgy.

Glossary

biblical inspiration
The process by which the Holy Spirit assisted the human writers of Sacred Scripture so that they would teach faithfully, and without error, the saving truth that God, the principal author of the Scriptures, wished to communicate.

Body of Christ
An image for the Church used by Saint Paul the Apostle that teaches that all the members of the Church are one in Christ, the Head of the Church, and that all members have a unique and vital work in the Church.

Chrism
Perfumed olive oil; one of the three oils blessed by the Church that is used in the celebration of Baptism, Confirmation, and Holy Orders, as well as in the consecration of churches, the altar, and sacred vessels.

Chrism Mass
The Mass celebrated during Holy Week, if possible on Holy Thursday morning, by the bishop of a diocese who consecrates the sacred Chrism and other oils that will be used at liturgies in every church of the diocese throughout the year.

Covenant
The solemn agreement between God and his people in which they mutually committed themselves to each other; the new and everlasting Covenant was established in Jesus Christ through his Paschal Mystery—the saving mystery of his Passion, death, Resurrection, and Ascension—and the sending of the Holy Spirit on Pentecost.

Church
The People of God, whom God the Father has called together in Jesus Christ through the power of the Holy Spirit. The word *church* comes from the Greek word *ekklesia* meaning "convocation, a calling together." The Church is the sacrament of Salvation, the sign and instrument of our reconciliation and communion with God and with one another. The Church is the Body of Christ, the Bride of Christ, and the Temple of the Holy Spirit.

Divine Revelation
God's free gift of gradually, over time, communicating in words and deeds his own mystery and his divine plan of creation and Salvation.

epiclesis
The name given to the prayer that invokes the transforming presence of the Holy Spirit.

encyclical
A formal letter about doctrinal or moral teaching or another aspect of the life of the Church written by the Pope or under the authority of the Pope.

evangelization
The central work of the Church for which she exists; the Church's work of sharing the Gospel with all people "so that it may enter the hearts of all [people] and renew the face of the earth."

Kingdom of God
The biblical image used to describe all people and creation living in communion with God when Jesus Christ comes again in glory at the end of time.

Lectionary
The book that contains the Scripture readings that are assigned to be proclaimed at the celebration of the liturgy.

liturgy
The participation of the People of God in the "work of God"—the work of the whole Church, of Christ the Head of the Church, and of the members of the Body of Christ through which Christ continues his work of Redemption. The word *liturgy* comes from a Greek word meaning "a public work done on behalf of the people."

Liturgy of the Word
The part of the Church's liturgical celebrations during which the Sacred Scriptures are proclaimed and the assembly of the faithful is invited to respond with faith.

Mass
A word meaning "sent forth"; the main sacramental celebration of the Church at which we gather to listen to the Word of God and celebrate the Eucharist; the name given to the Eucharistic celebration coming from the Latin words of one of the closing dismissals, "*Ite, missa est.*"

Messiah
The Hebrew word *messiah* is translated into Greek as *christos* (Christ) and means "anointed one"; the Anointed One whom God promised to send his people to save them; Jesus Christ, the Anointed One of God.

parable
A type of story that Jesus told comparing one thing to another to teach and invite his listeners to make a decision to live for the Kingdom of God.

Paschal Mystery
The saving events of the Passion, death, Resurrection, and glorious Ascension of Jesus Christ.

Passover
The Jewish feast that celebrates the sparing of the Israelites from death, and God's saving his people from slavery in Egypt and leading them to freedom in the land he promised them.

Period of Purification and Enlightenment
The last stage of the catechumenal process in the rite of Christian Initiation, which coincides with the Season of Lent.

Pharisee
A member of a Jewish sect in Jesus' time whose members dedicated their lives to the strict keeping of the Law found in the Torah.

prefigure
A word meaning "to figure, or image, or announce beforehand."

Resurrection
The bodily raising of Jesus from the dead on the third day of his death on the cross and burial in a tomb to a new and glorified life, an event historically attested to by the disciples who really encountered the Risen One.

sacrament
A efficacious sign of grace, instituted by Christ and entrusted to the Church, by which divine life is dispensed to us through the work of the Holy Spirit.

Sacraments of Christian Initiation
Baptism, Confirmation, and Eucharist; the foundation of every Christian life.

sacrifice
The free offering, out of love, of something of great value, for example, one's life.

Sanhedrin
The supreme governing council of the Jewish people during Jesus' time.

scapegoat
A term that refers to an individual who carries the blame or guilt of others; originally an animal on whom the Jewish High Priest laid hands in a ritual ceremony, transferring the guilt of the Israelite people, then banishing the animal to the desert so that it would "carry away" the people's sins.

Servant poems
A series of passages in the Book of Isaiah that describe the sufferings of the Servant of YHWH who will redeem God's people.

Shalom
Hebrew word for *peace*, the sum of all blessings, material and spiritual, and a state of harmony with God, self, and nature that brings a person perfect happiness.

Sign of Peace
One of the Church's most ancient liturgical rituals in which Christians share with one another a gesture and a prayer that the blessings of Christ's peace come upon them.

Viaticum
The name given to Holy Communion when it is administered to a dying person as food and strength for their journey from life on earth, through death, to eternal life.

Index

Credits

Scripture excerpts are taken or adapted from the *New American Bible with Revised New Testament and Psalms* Copyright © 1991, 1986, 1970, Confraternity of Christian Doctrine, Washington, DC. Used with permission. All rights reserved. No part of the *New American Bible* may be reproduced by any means without the permission of the copyright owner.

Excerpts from the English translation of the *Catechism of the Catholic Church* for use in the United States of America, second edition, copyright © 1997, United States Catholic Conference, Inc.–Libreria Editrice Vaticana. Used with permission.

Excerpts from the English translation of *The Roman Missal* © 1973, International Committee on English in the Liturgy, Inc. ICEL; excerpts from English translation of the *Rite of Baptism for Children* © 1969, ICEL; the English translation of the Prayer of the Penitent from *Rite of Penance* © 1974, ICEL; excerpts from the English translation of *Rite of Confirmation (Second Edition)* © 1975, ICEL; excerpts from the English translation of *A Book of Prayers* © 1982, ICEL; excerpts from the English translation of *The General Instruction of the Roman Missal* (Third Typical Edition) © 2002, ICEL. All rights reserved.

English translation of "The Nicene Creed," "The Apostles' Creed," "Sanctus," "Benedictus," "Gloria Patri," and "Magnificat" by the International Consultation on English Texts (ICET).

Excerpts from *The Constitution on the Sacred Liturgy (Sacrosanctum Concilium)* from *Vatican Council II: The Conciliar and Post Conciliar Documents*, New Revised Edition, Austin Flannery, O.P., Gen. Ed., copyright © 1975, 1986, 1992, 1996 by Costello Publishing Company, Inc. Used with Permission.

Excerpts from *Catecheses Mystigogicae*, Saint Cyril of Jerusalem.

Cover design: Kristy Howard

PHOTO CREDITS
Abbreviated as follows: (bkgd) background, (t) top, (b) bottom, (l) left, (r) right, (c) center.

Page 4, © Gene Plaisted, OSC/Crosiers; 5, © Michael Sohn/AP Wideworld; 6, © SuperStock, Inc./SuperStock; 7, © Beauvais Cathedral, Beauvais, France/Giraudon/ The Bridgeman Art Library; 8–9, © Bill Wittman/ Wittman; 10, © Gene Plaisted, OSC/ Crosiers; 11, © Bill Wittman/Wittman; 12–13 (all), courtesy of Encounter the Gospel of Life Organization; 14 (tl), © Photodisc/ Punchstock; 14 (r), © Farida Zaman/Images.com; 15 (t), © Ron Chapple/Getty Images; 15 (b), © Photodisc/ Punchstock; 17, © Leon Zernitsky/Images.com; 18–19, © Bill Wittman/Wittman; 20, © Gene Plaisted, OSC/ Crosiers; 21, © Jose Ortega/Images.com; 22, © Bill Wittman/Wittman; 23, Midwest Theological Forum/ theologicalforum.org; 24 (tr), © Carlos Silva/AP Wideworld; 24 (bl), Courtesy of the Sisters of Notre Dame de Namur; 25 (all), © Paulo Santos/AP Wideworld; 26, © Jose Ortega/Images.com; 26–27, © Comstock Images/Punchstock; 27, © Reed Kaestner/ Corbis; 30, 31, © SuperStock, Inc/SuperStock; 32, © Steve Kropp/Images.com; 33, © Julie Lonneman/The Spirit Source; 34, © RCL/RCL; 35, © Bill Wittman/ Wittman; 36–37 (all), © Jesuit Volunteer Corps/Jesuit Volunteer Corps; 38, © George Shewchuk/Getty Images; 41, © Julie Lonneman/The Spirit Source; 42, © SuperStock, Inc./SuperStock; 43, © Gene Plaisted, OSC/Crosiers; 44, © Bill Wittman/Wittman; 45, © Gene Plaisted, OSC/Crosiers; 47, © Bill Wittman/Wittman; 48, © The Granger Collection, New York; 49 (tr), © Massimo Sambucetti/AP Wideworld; 49 (bl), © C. Walker/Topham/The Image Works; 50 (tl), © Tony Freeman/PhotoEdit; 50 (br), © Getty Images/ Getty Images; 51 (bl), © Bob Elsdale/Getty Images; 51 (tr), © Dana White/PhotoEdit; 53–54, © Gene Plaisted, OSC/Crosiers; 56, ©, Bill Wittman/Wittman; 57, © Alan Oddie/PhotoEdit; 58, © Bill Wittman/Wittman; 60, Courtesy of Cristo Rey; 61 (all), Courtesy of Cristo Rey; 62, © Images.com/Corbis; 63, © Liz Couldwell/Susan Doyle/Getty Images; 65, © Pat LaCroix/Getty Images; 66, © Stephan Daigle/Images.com; 68, © Gene Plaisted, OSC/Crosiers; 69, © AP Wideworld; 70, © Gene Plaisted, OSC/Crosiers; 71, © Bill Wittman/Wittman; 72–73 (all), © Dan O'Connell/Peacebuilders Initiative; 74 (tl, c), © Design Pics/Design Pics; 74 (b), © Bill Wittman/ Wittman; 75, © Myrleen Ferguson Cate/PhotoEdit; 77, © Alex Wong/Getty Images; 78, © Dave Bartruff/Corbis; 79, © Mary Evans Picture Library/The Image Works; 80, © Gene Plaisted, OSC/Crosiers; 81, © Lawrence Jackson/AP Wideworld; 82–83, © Gene Plaisted, OSC/Crosiers; 83, © Bill Wittman/Wittman; 84 (tl), © ISSOUF SANOGO/AFP/Getty Images; 84–85, © Sean Sprague/The Image Works; 86 (t), © Encounter Gospel of Life/Encounter Gospel of Life Organization; 86 (b), © Journal-Courier/Steve/The Image Works; 89, © Diane Ong/Superstock; 90, © Gene Plaisted, OSC/Crosiers; 91, © SuperStock/SuperStock; 92 (t), © AP Wideworld; 92 (b), © Associated Press/AP Wideworld; 93, © USCCB/ USCCB; 94, © artservant/artservant; 95, © Gene Plaisted, OSC/Crosiers; 96 (tl), © Bill Wittman/Wittman; 96 (bl), PNCEA; 97, © Robin Nelson/PhotoEdit; 98 (t), © Carsten Koall/Getty Images; 98 (c), © Gaudenti Sergio/Kipa/Corbis; 99, © Jeff Greenberg/PhotoEdit.